Connected Mathematics 2

Growing, Growing, Growing

Exponential Relationships

2.7×10^{12}

Glenda Lappan

James T. Fey

William M. Fitzgerald

Susan N. Friel

Elizabeth Difanis Phillips

PEARSON

Boston, Massachusetts · Glenview, Illinois · Shoreview, Minnesota · Upper Saddle River, New Jersey

Connected Mathematics™ was developed at Michigan State University with financial support from the Michigan State University Office of the Provost, Computing and Technology, and the College of Natural Science.

This material is based upon work supported by the National Science Foundation under Grant No. MDR 9150217 and Grant No. ESI 9986372. Opinions expressed are those of the authors and not necessarily those of the Foundation.

The Michigan State University authors and administration have agreed that all MSU royalties arising from this publication will be devoted to purposes supported by the MSU Mathematics Education Enrichment Fund.

Acknowledgments appear on page 86, which constitutes an extension of this copyright page.

13-digit ISBN 978-0-13-366151-4
10-digit ISBN 0-13-366151-2
2 3 4 5 6 7 8 9 10   11 10 09 08

Authors of Connected Mathematics

(from left to right) Glenda Lappan, Betty Phillips, Susan Friel, Bill Fitzgerald, Jim Fey

Glenda Lappan is a University Distinguished Professor in the Department of Mathematics at Michigan State University. Her research and development interests are in the connected areas of students' learning of mathematics and mathematics teachers' professional growth and change related to the development and enactment of K–12 curriculum materials.

James T. Fey is a Professor of Curriculum and Instruction and Mathematics at the University of Maryland. His consistent professional interest has been development and research focused on curriculum materials that engage middle and high school students in problem-based collaborative investigations of mathematical ideas and their applications.

William M. Fitzgerald *(Deceased)* was a Professor in the Department of Mathematics at Michigan State University. His early research was on the use of concrete materials in supporting student learning and led to the development of teaching materials for laboratory environments. Later he helped develop a teaching model to support student experimentation with mathematics.

Susan N. Friel is a Professor of Mathematics Education in the School of Education at the University of North Carolina at Chapel Hill. Her research interests focus on statistics education for middle-grade students and, more broadly, on teachers' professional development and growth in teaching mathematics K–8.

Elizabeth Difanis Phillips is a Senior Academic Specialist in the Mathematics Department of Michigan State University. She is interested in teaching and learning mathematics for both teachers and students. These interests have led to curriculum and professional development projects at the middle school and high school levels, as well as projects related to the teaching and learning of algebra across the grades.

Field Test Sites for CMP2

During the development of the revised edition of *Connected Mathematics* (CMP2), more than 100 classroom teachers have field-tested materials at 49 school sites in 12 states and the District of Columbia. This classroom testing occurred over three academic years (2001 through 2004), allowing careful study of the effectiveness of each of the 24 units that comprise the program. A special thanks to the students and teachers at these pilot schools.

Arkansas
Magnolia Public Schools
Kittena Bell*, Judith Trowell*; *Central Elementary School:* Maxine Broom, Betty Eddy, Tiffany Fallin, Bonnie Flurry, Carolyn Monk, Elizabeth Tye; *Magnolia Junior High School:* Monique Bryan, Ginger Cook, David Graham, Shelby Lamkin

Colorado
Boulder Public Schools
Nevin Platt Middle School: Judith Koenig
St. Vrain Valley School District, Longmont
Westview Middle School: Colleen Beyer, Kitty Canupp, Ellie Decker*, Peggy McCarthy, Tanya deNobrega, Cindy Payne, Ericka Pilon, Andrew Roberts

District of Columbia
Capitol Hill Day School: Ann Lawrence

Georgia
University of Georgia, Athens
Brad Findell
Madison Public Schools
Morgan County Middle School: Renee Burgdorf, Lynn Harris, Nancy Kurtz, Carolyn Stewart

Maine
Falmouth Public Schools
Falmouth Middle School: Donna Erikson, Joyce Hebert, Paula Hodgkins, Rick Hogan, David Legere, Cynthia Martin, Barbara Stiles, Shawn Towle*

Michigan
Portland Public Schools
Portland Middle School: Mark Braun, Holly DeRosia, Kathy Dole*, Angie Foote, Teri Keusch, Tammi Wardwell
Traverse City Area Public Schools
Bertha Vos Elementary: Kristin Sak; *Central Grade School:* Michelle Clark; Jody Meyers; *Eastern Elementary:* Karrie Tufts; *Interlochen Elementary:* Mary McGee-Cullen; *Long Lake Elementary:* Julie Faulkner*, Charlie Maxbauer, Katherine Sleder; *Norris Elementary:* Hope Slanaker; *Oak Park Elementary:* Jessica Steed; *Traverse Heights Elementary:* Jennifer Wolfert; *Westwoods Elementary:* Nancy Conn; *Old Mission Peninsula School:* Deb Larimer; *Traverse City East Junior High:* Ivanka Berkshire, Ruthanne Kladder, Jan Palkowski, Jane Peterson, Mary Beth Schmitt; *Traverse City West Junior High:* Dan Fouch*, Ray Fouch
Sturgis Public Schools
Sturgis Middle School: Ellen Eisele

Minnesota
Burnsville School District 191
Hidden Valley Elementary: Stephanie Cin, Jane McDevitt
Hopkins School District 270
Alice Smith Elementary: Sandra Cowing, Kathleen Gustafson, Martha Mason, Scott Stillman; *Eisenhower Elementary:* Chad Bellig, Patrick Berger, Nancy Glades, Kye Johnson, Shane Wasserman, Victoria Wilson; *Gatewood Elementary:* Sarah Ham, Julie Kloos, Janine Pung, Larry Wade; *Glen Lake Elementary:* Jacqueline Cramer, Kathy Hering, Cecelia Morris,

Robb Trenda; *Katherine Curren Elementary:* Diane Bancroft, Sue DeWit, John Wilson; *L. H. Tanglen Elementary:* Kevin Athmann, Lisa Becker, Mary LaBelle, Kathy Rezac, Roberta Severson; *Meadowbrook Elementary:* Jan Gauger, Hildy Shank, Jessica Zimmerman; *North Junior High:* Laurel Hahn, Kristin Lee, Jodi Markuson, Bruce Mestemacher, Laurel Miller, Bonnie Rinker, Jeannine Salzer, Sarah Shafer, Cam Stottler; *West Junior High:* Alicia Beebe, Kristie Earl, Nobu Fujii, Pam Georgetti, Susan Gilbert, Regina Nelson Johnson, Debra Lindstrom, Michele Luke*, Jon Sorenson
Minneapolis School District 1
Ann Sullivan K-8 School: Bronwyn Collins; Anne Bartel* (Curriculum and Instruction Office)
Wayzata School District 284
Central Middle School: Sarajane Myers, Dan Nielsen, Tanya Ravenholdt
White Bear Lake School District 624
Central Middle School: Amy Jorgenson, Michelle Reich, Brenda Sammon

New York
New York City Public Schools
IS 89: Yelena Aynbinder, Chi-Man Ng, Nina Rapaport, Joel Spengler, Phyllis Tam*, Brent Wyso; *Wagner Middle School:* Jason Appel, Intissar Fernandez, Yee Gee Get, Richard Goldstein, Irving Marcus, Sue Norton, Bernadita Owens, Jennifer Rehn*, Kevin Yuhas

---

* indicates a Field Test Site Coordinator

Ohio
Talawanda School District, Oxford
Talawanda Middle School: Teresa Abrams, Larry Brock, Heather Brosey, Julie Churchman, Monna Even, Karen Fitch, Bob George, Amanda Klee, Pat Meade, Sandy Montgomery, Barbara Sherman, Lauren Steidl

Miami University
Jeffrey Wanko*

Springfield Public Schools
Rockway School: Jim Mamer

Pennsylvania
Pittsburgh Public Schools
Kenneth Labuskes, Marianne O'Connor, Mary Lynn Raith*; *Arthur J. Rooney Middle School:* David Hairston, Stamatina Mousetis, Alfredo Zangaro; *Frick International Studies Academy:* Suzanne Berry, Janet Falkowski, Constance Finseth, Romika Hodge, Frank Machi; *Reizenstein Middle School:* Jeff Baldwin, James Brautigam, Lorena Burnett, Glen Cobbett, Michael Jordan, Margaret Lazur, Melissa Munnell, Holly Neely, Ingrid Reed, Dennis Reft

Texas
Austin Independent School District
Bedichek Middle School: Lisa Brown, Jennifer Glasscock, Vicki Massey

El Paso Independent School District
Cordova Middle School: Armando Aguirre, Anneliesa Durkes, Sylvia Guzman, Pat Holguin*, William Holguin, Nancy Nava, Laura Orozco, Michelle Peña, Roberta Rosen, Patsy Smith, Jeremy Wolf

Plano Independent School District
Patt Henry, James Wohlgehagen*; *Frankford Middle School:* Mandy Baker, Cheryl Butsch, Amy Dudley, Betsy Eshelman, Janet Greene, Cort Haynes, Kathy Letchworth, Kay Marshall, Kelly McCants, Amy Reck, Judy Scott, Syndy Snyder, Lisa Wang; *Wilson Middle School:* Darcie Bane, Amanda Bedenko, Whitney Evans, Tonelli Hatley, Sarah (Becky) Higgs, Kelly Johnston, Rebecca McElligott, Kay Neuse, Cheri Slocum, Kelli Straight

Washington
Evergreen School District
Shahala Middle School: Nicole Abrahamsen, Terry Coon*, Carey Doyle, Sheryl Drechsler, George Gemma, Gina Helland, Amy Hilario, Darla Lidyard, Sean McCarthy, Tilly Meyer, Willow Neuwelt, Todd Parsons, Brian Pederson, Stan Posey, Shawn Scott, Craig Sjoberg, Lynette Sundstrom, Charles Switzer, Luke Youngblood

Wisconsin
Beaver Dam Unified School District
Beaver Dam Middle School: Jim Braemer, Jeanne Frick, Jessica Greatens, Barbara Link, Dennis McCormick, Karen Michels, Nancy Nichols*, Nancy Palm, Shelly Stelsel, Susan Wiggins

---

* indicates a Field Test Site Coordinator

Reviews of CMP to Guide Development of CMP2

Before writing for CMP2 began or field tests were conducted, the first edition of *Connected Mathematics* was submitted to the mathematics faculties of school districts from many parts of the country and to 80 individual reviewers for extensive comments.

School District Survey Reviews of CMP

Arizona
Madison School District #38 (Phoenix)

Arkansas
Cabot School District, Little Rock School District, Magnolia School District

California
Los Angeles Unified School District

Colorado
St. Vrain Valley School District (Longmont)

Florida
Leon County Schools (Tallahassee)

Illinois
School District #21 (Wheeling)

Indiana
Joseph L. Block Junior High (East Chicago)

Kentucky
Fayette County Public Schools (Lexington)

Maine
Selection of Schools

Massachusetts
Selection of Schools

Michigan
Sparta Area Schools

Minnesota
Hopkins School District

Texas
Austin Independent School District, The El Paso Collaborative for Academic Excellence, Plano Independent School District

Wisconsin
Platteville Middle School

Individual Reviewers of CMP

Arkansas
Deborah Cramer; Robby Frizzell *(Taylor)*; Lowell Lynde *(University of Arkansas, Monticello)*; Leigh Manzer *(Norfork)*; Lynne Roberts *(Emerson High School, Emerson)*; Tony Timms *(Cabot Public Schools)*; Judith Trowell *(Arkansas Department of Higher Education)*

California
José Alcantar *(Gilroy)*; Eugenie Belcher *(Gilroy)*; Marian Pasternack *(Lowman M. S. T. Center, North Hollywood)*; Susana Pezoa *(San Jose)*; Todd Rabusin *(Hollister)*; Margaret Siegfried *(Ocala Middle School, San Jose)*; Polly Underwood *(Ocala Middle School, San Jose)*

Colorado
Janeane Golliher *(St. Vrain Valley School District, Longmont)*; Judith Koenig *(Nevin Platt Middle School, Boulder)*

Florida
Paige Loggins *(Swift Creek Middle School, Tallahassee)*

Illinois
Jan Robinson *(School District #21, Wheeling)*

Indiana
Frances Jackson *(Joseph L. Block Junior High, East Chicago)*

Kentucky
Natalee Feese *(Fayette County Public Schools, Lexington)*

Maine
Betsy Berry *(Maine Math & Science Alliance, Augusta)*

Maryland
Joseph Gagnon *(University of Maryland, College Park)*; Paula Maccini *(University of Maryland, College Park)*

Massachusetts
George Cobb *(Mt. Holyoke College, South Hadley)*; Cliff Kanold *(University of Massachusetts, Amherst)*

Michigan
Mary Bouck *(Farwell Area Schools)*; Carol Dorer *(Slauson Middle School, Ann Arbor)*; Carrie Heaney *(Forsythe Middle School, Ann Arbor)*; Ellen Hopkins *(Clague Middle School, Ann Arbor)*; Teri Keusch *(Portland Middle School, Portland)*; Valerie Mills *(Oakland Schools, Waterford)*; Mary Beth Schmitt *(Traverse City East Junior High, Traverse City)*; Jack Smith *(Michigan State University, East Lansing)*; Rebecca Spencer *(Sparta Middle School, Sparta)*; Ann Marie Nicoll Turner *(Tappan Middle School, Ann Arbor)*; Scott Turner *(Scarlett Middle School, Ann Arbor)*

Minnesota
Margarita Alvarez *(Olson Middle School, Minneapolis)*; Jane Amundson *(Nicollet Junior High, Burnsville)*; Anne Bartel *(Minneapolis Public Schools)*; Gwen Ranzau Campbell *(Sunrise Park Middle School, White Bear Lake)*; Stephanie Cin *(Hidden Valley Elementary, Burnsville)*; Joan Garfield *(University of Minnesota, Minneapolis)*; Gretchen Hall *(Richfield Middle School, Richfield)*; Jennifer Larson *(Olson Middle School, Minneapolis)*; Michele Luke *(West Junior High, Minnetonka)*; Jeni Meyer *(Richfield Junior High, Richfield)*; Judy Pfingsten *(Inver Grove Heights Middle School, Inver Grove Heights)*; Sarah Shafer *(North Junior High, Minnetonka)*; Genni Steele *(Central Middle School, White Bear Lake)*; Victoria Wilson *(Eisenhower Elementary, Hopkins)*; Paul Zorn *(St. Olaf College, Northfield)*

New York
Debra Altenau-Bartolino *(Greenwich Village Middle School, New York)*; Doug Clements *(University of Buffalo)*; Francis Curcio *(New York University, New York)*; Christine Dorosh *(Clinton School for Writers, Brooklyn)*; Jennifer Rehn *(East Side Middle School, New York)*; Phyllis Tam *(IS 89 Lab School, New York)*;

Marie Turini *(Louis Armstrong Middle School, New York)*; Lucy West *(Community School District 2, New York)*; Monica Witt *(Simon Baruch Intermediate School 104, New York)*

Pennsylvania
Robert Aglietti *(Pittsburgh)*; Sharon Mihalich *(Pittsburgh)*; Jennifer Plumb *(South Hills Middle School, Pittsburgh)*; Mary Lynn Raith *(Pittsburgh Public Schools)*

Texas
Michelle Bittick *(Austin Independent School District)*; Margaret Cregg *(Plano Independent School District)*; Sheila Cunningham *(Klein Independent School District)*; Judy Hill *(Austin Independent School District)*; Patricia Holguin *(El Paso Independent School District)*; Bonnie McNemar *(Arlington)*; Kay Neuse *(Plano Independent School District)*; Joyce Polanco *(Austin Independent School District)*; Marge Ramirez *(University of Texas at El Paso)*; Pat Rossman *(Baker Campus, Austin)*; Cindy Schimek *(Houston)*; Cynthia Schneider *(Charles A. Dana Center, University of Texas at Austin)*; Uri Treisman *(Charles A. Dana Center, University of Texas at Austin)*; Jacqueline Weilmuenster *(Grapevine-Colleyville Independent School District)*; LuAnn Weynand *(San Antonio)*; Carmen Whitman *(Austin Independent School District)*; James Wohlgehagen *(Plano Independent School District)*

Washington
Ramesh Gangolli *(University of Washington, Seattle)*

Wisconsin
Susan Lamon *(Marquette University, Hales Corner)*; Steve Reinhart *(retired, Chippewa Falls Middle School, Eau Claire)*

Table of Contents

Growing, Growing, Growing
Exponential Relationships

Growing, Growing, Growing

Exponential Relationships

When the water hyacinth was introduced to Lake Victoria, it spread quickly over the lake's surface. At one point, the plant covered 769 square miles, and its area was doubling every 15 days. What equation models this growth?

When Sam was in seventh grade, his aunt gave him a stamp collection worth $2,500. The value of the collection increased by 6% each year for several years in a row. What was the value of Sam's collection after four years?

What pattern of change would you expect to find in the temperature of a hot drink as time passes? What would a graph of the (time, drink temperature) data look like?

One of the most important uses of algebra is to model patterns of change. You are already familiar with linear patterns of change. Linear patterns have constant differences and straight-line graphs. In a linear relationship, the y-value increases by a constant amount each time the x-value increases by 1.

In this unit, you will study exponential patterns of change.

Exponential growth patterns are fascinating because, although the values may change gradually at first, they eventually increase very rapidly. Patterns that decrease, or decay, exponentially may decrease quickly at first, but eventually they decrease very slowly.

As you work through the investigations in this unit, you will encounter problems like those the on the facing page.

Mathematical Highlights

Exponential Relationships

In *Growing, Growing, Growing,* you will explore exponential relationships, one of the most important types of nonlinear relationships.

You will learn how to

- Identify situations in which a quantity grows or decays exponentially
- Recognize the connections between exponential equations and the growth patterns in tables and graphs of those equations
- Construct equations to express exponential patterns in data tables, graphs, and problem situations
- Solve problems about exponential growth and decay from a variety of different areas, including science and business
- Compare exponential and linear relationships
- Understand the rules for working with exponents

As you work on the problems in this unit, ask yourself questions about situations that involve nonlinear relationships:

What are the variables?

Is the relationship between variables an example of exponential growth or decay?

How can the relationship be detected in a table, graph, or equation?

What is the growth or decay factor?

What equation models the data in the table?

What equation models the pattern in the graph?

What can I learn about this situation by studying a table, graph, or equation of the exponential relationship?

How does the relationship compare to other types of relationships that I have studied?

Investigation 1

Exponential Growth

In this investigation, you will explore *exponential growth* as you cut paper in half over and over and read about a very smart peasant from the ancient kingdom of Montarek. You will compare exponential growth with linear growth. You will also explore exponential patterns in tables, graphs, and equations.

1.1 Making Ballots

Chen, the secretary of the Student Government Association, is making ballots for tonight's meeting. He starts by cutting a sheet of paper in half. He then stacks the two pieces and cuts them in half. He stacks the resulting four pieces and cuts them in half. He repeats this process, creating smaller and smaller pieces of paper.

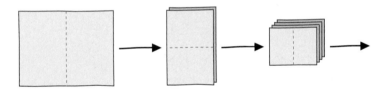

After each cut, Chen counts the ballots and records the results in a table.

Number of Cuts	Number of Ballots
1	2
2	4
3	
4	

Chen wants to predict the number of ballots after any number of cuts.

A. Make a table to show the number of ballots after each of the first five cuts.

B. Look for a pattern in the way the number of ballots changes with each cut. Use your observations to extend your table to show the number of ballots for up to 10 cuts.

C. Suppose Chen could make 20 cuts. How many ballots would he have? How many ballots would he have if he could make 30 cuts?

D. How many cuts would it take to make enough ballots for all 500 students at Chen's school?

ACE Homework starts on page 11.

1.2 Requesting a Reward

When you found the number of ballots after 10, 20, and 30 cuts, you may have multiplied long strings of 2s. Instead of writing long product strings of the same factor, you can use **exponential form.** For example, you can write $2 \times 2 \times 2 \times 2 \times 2$ as 2^5, which is read "2 to the fifth power."

In the expression 2^5, 5 is the **exponent** and 2 is the **base.** When you evaluate 2^5, you get $2^5 = 2 \times 2 \times 2 \times 2 \times 2 = 32$. We say that 32 is the **standard form** for 2^5.

Getting Ready for Problem 1.2

- Write each expression in exponential form.

  a. $2 \times 2 \times 2$ **b.** $5 \times 5 \times 5 \times 5$

  c. $1.5 \cdot 1.5 \cdot 1.5 \cdot 1.5 \cdot 1.5 \cdot 1.5 \cdot 1.5$

- Write each expression in standard form.

  a. 2^7 **b.** 3^3 **c.** 4.2^3

- Most calculators have a ⚲ or ⚲ key for evaluating exponents. Use your calculator to find the standard form for each expression.

  a. 2^{15} **b.** 3^{10} **c.** 1.5^{20}

- Explain how the meanings of $5^2, 2^5$, and 5×2 differ.

One day in the ancient kingdom of Montarek, a peasant saved the life of the king's daughter. The king was so grateful he told the peasant she could have any reward she desired. The peasant—who was also the kingdom's chess champion—made an unusual request:

"I would like you to place 1 ruba on the first square of my chessboard, 2 rubas on the second square, 4 on the third square, 8 on the fourth square, and so on, until you have covered all 64 squares. Each square should have twice as many rubas as the previous square."

The king replied, "Rubas are the least valuable coin in the kingdom. Surely you can think of a better reward." But the peasant insisted, so the king agreed to her request. *Did the peasant make a wise choice?*

Problem 1.2 Representing Exponential Relationships

A. 1. Make a table showing the number of rubas the king will place on squares 1 through 10 of the chessboard.

   2. How does the number of rubas change from one square to the next?

B. Graph the (*number of the square, number of rubas*) data for squares 1 to 10.

C. Write an equation for the relationship between the number of the square n and the number of rubas r.

D. How does the pattern of change you observed in the table show up in the graph? How does it show up in the equation?

E. Which square will have 2^{30} rubas? Explain.

F. What is the first square on which the king will place at least one million rubas? How many rubas will be on this square?

ACE Homework starts on page 11.

The patterns of change in the number of ballots in Problem 1.1 and in the number of rubas in Problem 1.2 show **exponential growth.** These relationships are called **exponential relationships.** In each case, you can find the value for any square or cut by multiplying the value for the previous square or cut by a fixed number. This fixed number is called the **growth factor.**

- What are the growth factors for the situations in Problems 1.1 and 1.2?

The king told the queen about the reward he had promised the peasant. The queen said, "You have promised her more money than we have in the entire royal treasury! You must convince her to accept a different reward."

After much thought, the king came up with Plan 2. He would make a new board with only 16 squares. He would place 1 ruba on the first square and 3 rubas on the second. He drew a graph to show the number of rubas on the first five squares. He would continue this pattern until all 16 squares were filled.

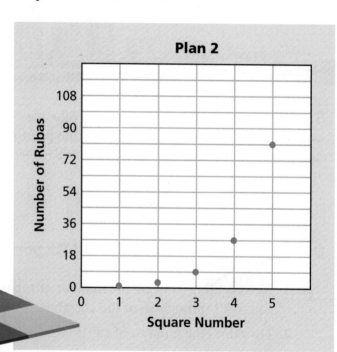

The queen wasn't convinced about the king's new plan, so she devised a third plan. Under Plan 3, the king would make a board with 12 squares. He would place 1 ruba on the first square. He would use the equation $r = 4^{n-1}$ to figure out how many rubas to put on each of the other squares. In the equation, r is the number of rubas on square n.

A. In the table below, Plan 1 is the reward requested by the peasant. Plan 2 is the king's new plan. Plan 3 is the queen's plan. Copy and extend the table to show the number of rubas on squares 1 to 10 for each plan.

Reward Plans

Square Number	Number of Rubas		
	Plan 1	Plan 2	Plan 3
1	1	1	1
2	2	3	4
3	4	▪	▪
4	▪	▪	▪

B. 1. How are the patterns of change in the number of rubas under Plans 2 and 3 similar to and different from the pattern of change for Plan 1?

2. Are the growth patterns for Plans 2 and 3 exponential relationships? If so, what is the growth factor for each?

C. Write an equation for the relationship between the number of the square n and the number of rubas r for Plan 2.

D. Make a graph of Plan 3 for $n = 1$ to 10. How does your graph compare to the graphs for Plans 1 and 2?

E. The queen's assistant wrote the equation $r = \frac{1}{4}(4^n)$ for Plan 3. This equation is different from the one the queen wrote. Did the assistant make a mistake? Explain.

F. For each plan, how many rubas would be on the final square?

ACE Homework starts on page 11.

Before presenting Plans 2 and 3 to the peasant, the king consulted with his financial advisors. They told him that either plan would devastate the royal treasury.

The advisors proposed a fourth plan. Under Plan 4, the king would put 20 rubas on the first square of a chessboard, 25 on the second, 30 on the third, and so on. He would increase the number of rubas by 5 for each square, until all 64 squares were covered.

To help persuade the peasant to accept their plan, the advisors prepared the following table for the first six squares. The king presented the plan to the peasant and gave her a day to consider the offer.

Reward Plans

Square Number	Number of Rubas	
	Plan 1	Plan 4
1	1	20
2	2	25
3	4	30
4	8	35
5	16	40
6	32	45

Do you think the peasant should accept the new plan? Explain.

Problem 1.4 **Comparing Growth Patterns**

A. Is the growth pattern in Plan 4 an exponential relationship? Explain.

B. Describe the graph of Plan 4 and compare it to the graph of Plan 1.

C. 1. Write an equation for the relationship between the number of the square n and the number of rubas r for Plan 4.

 2. Compare this equation to the equation for Plan 1.

 3. How is the change in the number of rubas from one square to the next shown in the equations for Plan 1 and Plan 4?

D. For Plans 1 and 4, how many rubas would be on square 20? How many rubas would be on square 21?

ACE Homework starts on page 11.

Applications

1. Cut a sheet of paper into thirds. Stack the three pieces and cut the stack into thirds. Stack all the pieces and cut the stack into thirds again.

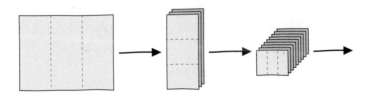

a. Copy and complete this table to show the number of ballots after each of the first five cuts.

Number of Cuts	Number of Ballots
1	3
2	▨
3	▨
4	▨
5	▨

b. Suppose you continued this process. How many ballots would you have after 10 cuts? How many would you have after n cuts?

c. How many cuts would it take to make at least one million ballots?

Write each expression in exponential form.

2. $2 \times 2 \times 2 \times 2$

3. $10 \cdot 10 \cdot 10 \cdot 10 \cdot 10 \cdot 10 \cdot 10$

4. $2.5 \times 2.5 \times 2.5 \times 2.5 \times 2.5$

Write each expression in standard form.

5. 2^{10} **6.** 10^2 **7.** 3^9

8. You know that $5^2 = 25$. Use this fact to evaluate 5^4.

9. The standard form for 5^{14} is 6,103,515,625. Use this fact to evaluate 5^{15}.

10. Multiple Choice Which expression is equal to one million?

    A. 10^6 **B.** 6^{10} **C.** 100^2 **D.** 2^{100}

11. Use exponents to write an expression for one billion (1,000,000,000).

Decide whether each number is greater or less than one million *without using a calculator*. Try to decide without actually multiplying. Explain how you found your answer. Use a calculator to check whether you are right.

12. 9^6 **13.** 3^{10} **14.** 11^6

For Exercises 15–20, write the number in exponential form using 2, 3, 4, or 5 as the base.

15. 125   **16.** 64   **17.** 81

18. 3,125   **19.** 1,024   **20.** 4,096

Go Online
PHSchool.com

For: Multiple-Choice Skills Practice
Web Code: apa-3154

21. While studying her family's history, Angie discovers records of ancestors 12 generations back. She wonders how many ancestors she has had in the past 12 generations. She starts to make a diagram to help her figure this out. The diagram soon becomes very complex.

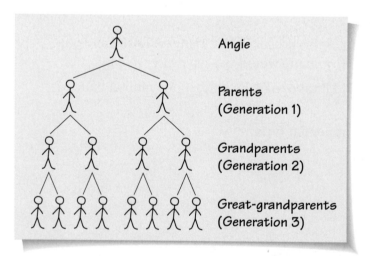

    a. Make a table and a graph showing the number of ancestors in each of the 12 generations.

    b. Write an equation for the number of ancestors a in a given generation n.

    c. What is the total number of ancestors in all 12 generations?

22. Many single-celled organisms reproduce by dividing into two identical cells. Suppose an amoeba (uh MEE buh) splits into two amoebas every half hour.

   a. An experiment starts with one amoeba. Make a table showing the number of amoebas at the end of each hour over an 8-hour period.

   b. Write an equation for the number of amoebas a after t hours.

   c. After how many hours will the number of amoebas reach one million?

   d. Make a graph of the (*time, amoebas*) data from part (a).

   e. What similarities do you notice in the pattern of change for the number of amoebas and the patterns of change for other problems in this investigation? What differences do you notice?

23. Zak's wealthy uncle wants to donate money to Zak's school for new computers. He suggests three possible plans for his donations.

Homework Help Online
PHSchool.com
For: Help with Exercise 23
Web Code: ape-3123

Plan 1: He will continue the pattern in this table until day 12.

Day	1	2	3	4
Donation	$1	$2	$4	$8

Plan 2: He will continue the pattern in this table until day 10.

Day	1	2	3	4
Donation	$1	$3	$9	$27

Plan 3: He will continue the pattern in this table until day 7.

Day	1	2	3	4
Donation	$1	$4	$16	$64

   a. Copy and extend each table to show how much money the school would receive each day.

   b. For each plan, write an equation for the relationship between the day number n and the number of dollars donated d.

   c. Which plan would give the school the greatest total amount of money?

   d. Zak says there is more than one equation for the relationship in Plan 1. He says that $d = 2^{n-1}$ and $d = \frac{1}{2}(2^n)$ both work. Is he correct? Are there two equations for each of the other plans?

24. Jenna is planning to swim in a charity swim-a-thon. Several relatives said they would sponsor her. Each of their donations is explained.

Grandmother: I will give you $1 if you swim 1 lap, $3 if you swim 2 laps, $5 if you swim 3 laps, $7 if you swim 4 laps, and so on.

Mother: I will give you $1 if you swim 1 lap, $3 if you swim 2 laps, $9 if you swim 3 laps, $27 if you swim 4 laps, and so on.

Aunt Lori: I will give you $2 if you swim 1 lap, $3.50 if you swim 2 laps, $5 if you swim 3 laps, $6.50 for 4 laps, and so on.

Uncle Jack: I will give you $1 if you swim 1 lap, $2 if you swim 2 laps, $4 if you swim 3 laps, $8 if you swim 4 laps, and so on.

a. Decide whether each donation pattern is *exponential*, *linear*, or *neither*.

b. For each relative, write an equation for the total donation *d* if Jenna swims *n* laps.

c. For each plan, tell how much money Jenna will raise if she swims 20 laps.

25. The graphs below represent $y = 2^x$ and $y = 2x + 1$.

    a. Tell which equation each graph represents. Explain your reasoning.

    b. The dashed segments show the vertical and horizontal change between points at equal x intervals. For each graph, compare the vertical and horizontal changes between pairs of points. What do you notice?

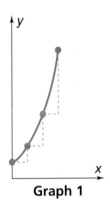

Graph 1

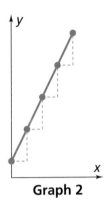

Graph 2

Study the pattern in each table.

    a. Tell whether the relationship between x and y is *linear, exponential,* or *neither*. **Explain your reasoning.**

    b. If the relationship is linear or exponential, give its equation.

26.

x	0	1	2	3	4	5
y	10	12.5	15	17.5	20	22.5

27.

x	0	1	2	3	4
y	1	6	36	216	1,296

28.

x	0	1	2	3	4	5	6	7	8
y	1	5	3	7	5	8	6	10	8

29.

x	0	1	2	3	4	5	6	7	8
y	2	4	8	16	32	64	128	256	512

30.

x	0	1	2	3	4	5
y	0	1	4	9	16	25

Connections

31. Refer to Problem 1.1. Suppose a stack of 250 sheets of paper is 1 inch high.

   a. How high would the stack of ballots be after 20 cuts? How high would it be after 30 cuts?

   b. How many cuts would it take to make a stack 1 foot high?

32. In Problem 1.2, suppose a Montarek ruba had the value of a modern U.S. penny. What would be the dollar values of the rubas on squares 10, 20, 30, 40, 50, and 60?

33. A ruba had the same thickness as a modern U.S. penny (about 0.06 inch). Suppose the king had been able to reward the peasant by using Plan 1 (doubling the number of rubas in each square).

   a. What would have been the height of the stack of rubas on square 64?

   b. The average distance from Earth to the moon is about 240,000 miles. Which (if any) of the stacks would have reached the moon?

34. One of the king's advisors suggested this plan: Put 100 rubas on the first square of a chessboard, 125 on the second square, 150 on the third square, and so on, increasing the number of rubas by 25 for each square.

   a. Write an equation for the numbers of rubas r on square n for this plan. Explain the meanings of the numbers and variables in your equation.

   b. Describe the graph of this plan.

   c. What is the total number of rubas on the first 10 squares? What is the total number on the first 20 squares?

For Exercises 35–37, find the slope and *y*-intercept of the graph of each equation.

35. $y = 3x - 10$ **36.** $y = 1.5 - 5.6x$ **37.** $y = 15 + \frac{2}{5}x$

38. Write an equation whose line is less steep than the line represented by $y = 15 + \frac{2}{5}x$.

39. Sarah used her calculator to keep track of the number of rubas in Problem 1.2. She found that there will be 2,147,483,648 rubas on square 32.

   a. How many rubas will be on square 33? How many will be on square 34? How many will be on square 35?

   b. Which square would have the number of rubas shown here?

      2,147,483,648 · 2 · 2 · 2 · 2 · 2 · 2 · 2 · 2 · 2

   c. Use your calculator to do the multiplication in part (b). Do you notice anything strange about the answer your calculator gives? Explain.

   d. Calculators use shorthand notation for showing very large numbers. For example, if you enter 10^12 on your calculator, you may get the result 1E12. This is shorthand for the number 1.0×10^{12}. The number 1.0×10^{12} is written in **scientific notation.** For a number to be in scientific notation, it must be in the form:

      (*a number greater than or equal to 1 but less than 10*) × (*a power of 10*)

      Write 2,147,483,648 · 2 · 2 · 2 · 2 · 2 · 2 · 2 · 2 · 2 in scientific notation.

   e. Write the numbers $2^{10}, 2^{20}, 2^{30}$, and 2^{35} in both standard and scientific notation.

   f. Explain how to write a large number in scientific notation.

Write each number in scientific notation.

40. 100,000,000   **41.** 29,678,900,500   **42.** 11,950,500,000,000

Find the largest whole-number value of *n* for which your calculator will display the result in standard notation.

43. 3^n **44.** π^n **45.** 12^n **46.** 237^n

Extensions

47. Consider these two equations:

      Equation 1: $r = 3^n - 1$ **Equation 2:** $r = 3^{n-1}$

   a. For each equation, find *r* when *n* is 2.

   b. For each equation, find *r* when *n* is 10.

   c. Explain why the equations give different values of *r* for the same value of *n*.

48. This table represents the number of ballots made by repeatedly cutting a sheet of paper in half four times. Assume the pattern continues.

Number of Cuts	Number of Ballots
1	2
2	4
3	8
4	16

a. Write an equation for the pattern in the table.

b. Use your equation and the table to determine the value of 2^0.

c. What do you think b^0 should equal for any number b? For example, what do you think 6^0 and 23^0 should equal? Explain.

49. When the king of Montarek tried to figure out the total number of rubas the peasant would receive under Plan 1, he noticed an interesting pattern.

a. Extend and complete this table for the first 10 squares.

Reward Plan 1

Square	Number of Rubas on Square	Total Number of Rubas
1	1	1
2	2	3
3	4	7
4	■	■

b. Describe the pattern of growth in the total number of rubas as the number of the square increases.

c. Write an equation for the relationship between the number of the square n and the total number of rubas t on the board.

d. When the total number of rubas reaches 1,000,000, how many squares will have been covered?

e. Suppose the king had been able to give the peasant the reward she requested. How many rubas would she have received?

50. Refer to Plans 1–4 in Problems 1.2 through 1.4.

a. Which plan should the king choose? Explain.

b. Which plan should the peasant choose? Explain.

c. Write an ending to the story of the king and the peasant.

Mathematical Reflections 1

In this investigation, you explored situations involving exponential growth. You saw how you could recognize patterns of exponential growth in tables, graphs, and equations.

Think about your answers to these questions. Discuss your ideas with other students and your teacher. Then write a summary of your findings in your notebook.

1. Describe an exponential growth pattern. Include key properties such as growth factors.

2. How are exponential growth patterns similar to and different from the linear growth patterns you worked with in earlier units?

Examining Growth Patterns

Now that you have learned to recognize exponential growth, you are ready to take a closer look at the tables, graphs, and equations of exponential relationships. You will explore this question:

How are the starting value and growth factor for an exponential relationship reflected in the table, graph, and equation?

Getting Ready for Problem 2.1

Students at West Junior High came up with two equations to represent the reward in Plan 1 of Investigation 1. Some students wrote $r = 2^{n-1}$ and others wrote $r = \frac{1}{2}(2^n)$. In both equations, r represents the number of rubas on square n.

- Are both equations correct? Explain.
- What is the value of r if $n = 1$? Does this make sense?
- What is the y-intercept for this relationship?

2.1 Killer Plant Strikes Lake Victoria

Exponential growth occurs in many real-life situations. For example, consider this story from 1998:

> **Water hyacinths, which experts say double in area every 5 to 15 days, are expanding across Africa's giant Lake Victoria. The foreign plant has taken over more than 769 square miles of the lake and is growing exponentially.**

"Killer Weed Strikes Lake Victoria" from *Christian Science Monitor*. January 12, 1998, Vol. 90, No. 32, p. 1.

Plants like the water hyacinth that grow and spread rapidly can affect native plants and fish. This in turn can affect the livelihood of fishermen. To understand how such plants grow, you will look at a similar situation.

Problem 2.1 *y*-Intercepts Other Than 1

Ghost Lake is a popular site for fishermen, campers, and boaters. In recent years, a certain water plant has been growing on the lake at an alarming rate. The surface area of Ghost Lake is 25,000,000 square feet. At present, 1,000 square feet are covered by the plant. The Department of Natural Resources estimates that the area is doubling every month.

A. 1. Write an equation that represents the growth pattern of the plant on Ghost Lake.

2. Explain what information the variables and numbers in your equation represent.

3. Compare this equation with the equations in Investigation 1.

B. 1. Make a graph of the equation.

2. How does this graph compare with the graphs of the exponential relationships in Investigation 1?

C. How much of the lake's surface will be covered with the water plant by the end of a year?

D. In how many months will the plant completely cover the surface of the lake?

ACE Homework starts on page 24.

Mold can spread rapidly. For example, the area covered by mold on a loaf of bread left out in warm weather grows exponentially.

Problem 2.2 Interpreting Exponential Equations

Students at Magnolia Middle School conducted an experiment. They set out a shallow pan containing a mixture of chicken bouillon (BOOL yahn), gelatin, and water. Each day, the students recorded the area of the mold in square millimeters.

The students wrote the exponential equation $m = 50(3^d)$ to model the growth of the mold. In this equation, m is the area of the mold in square millimeters after d days.

A. What is the area of the mold at the start of the experiment?

B. What is the growth factor?

C. What is the area of the mold after 5 days?

D. On which day will the area of the mold reach 6,400 mm^2?

E. An exponential equation can be written in the form $y = a(b^x)$, where a and b are constant values.

   1. What value does b have in the mold equation? What does this value represent?

   2. What value does a have in the mold equation? What does this value represent?

ACE Homework starts on page 24.

The graph shows the growth of a garter snake population after it was introduced to a new area. The population is growing exponentially.

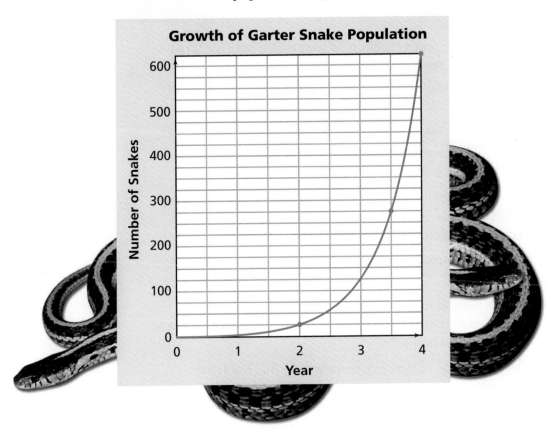

Growth of Garter Snake Population

Number of Snakes / Year

Problem 2.3 Interpreting Exponential Graphs

A. Explain how to find the growth factor for the population.

B. 1. Find the snake population for years 2, 3, and 4.

 2. Use the pattern in your answers from part (1) to estimate the population in year 1. Explain.

 3. Explain how you can find the *y*-intercept for the graph.

C. Write an equation relating time *t* in years and population *p*. Explain what information the numbers in the equation represent.

D. In what year is the population likely to reach 1,500?

ACE Homework starts on page 24.

Applications

1. If you don't brush your teeth regularly, it won't take long for large colonies of bacteria to grow in your mouth. Suppose a single bacterium lands on your tooth and starts multiplying by a factor of 4 every hour.

   a. Write an equation that describes the number of bacteria b in the new colony after n hours.

   b. How many bacteria will be in the colony after 7 hours?

   c. How many bacteria will be in the colony after 8 hours? Explain how you can find this answer by using the answer from part (b) instead of the equation.

   d. After how many hours will there be at least 1,000,000 bacteria in the colony?

   e. Suppose that, instead of 1 bacterium, 50 bacteria land in your mouth. Write an equation that describes the number of bacteria b in this colony after n hours.

   f. Under the conditions of part (e), there will be 3,276,800 bacteria in this new colony after 8 hours. How many bacteria will there be after 9 hours and after 10 hours? Explain how you can find these answers without using the equation from part (e).

2. Loon Lake has a "killer plant" problem similar to Ghost Lake in Problem 2.1. Currently, 5,000 square feet of the lake is covered with the plant. The area covered is growing by a factor of 1.5 each year.

   a. Copy and complete the table to show the area covered by the plant for the next 5 years.

   b. The surface area of the lake is approximately 200,000 square feet. How long will it take before the lake is completely covered?

Growth of Loon Lake Plant

Year	Area Covered (sq. ft)
0	5,000
1	■
2	■
3	■
4	■
5	■

3. Leaping Leonora just signed a contract with a women's basketball team. The contract guarantees her $20,000 the first year, $40,000 the second year, $80,000 the third year, $160,000 the fourth year, and so on, for 10 years.

a. Make a table showing Leonora's salary each year of this contract.

b. What total amount will Leonora earn over the 10 years?

c. Describe the growth pattern in Leonora's salary.

d. Write an equation for Leonora's salary *s* for any year *n* of her contract.

4. As a biology project, Talisha is studying the growth of a beetle population. She starts her experiment with 5 beetles. The next month she counts 15 beetles.

Homework
Help **O**nline
PHSchool.com
For: Help with Exercise 4
Web Code: ape-3204

a. Suppose the beetle population is growing linearly. How many beetles can Talisha expect to find after 2, 3, and 4 months?

b. Suppose the beetle population is growing exponentially. How many beetles can Talisha expect to find after 2, 3, and 4 months?

c. Write an equation for the number of beetles *b* after *m* months if the beetle population is growing linearly. Explain what information the variables and numbers represent.

d. Write an equation for the number of beetles *b* after *m* months if the beetle population is growing exponentially. Explain what information the variables and numbers represent.

e. How long will it take the beetle population to reach 200 if it is growing linearly?

f. How long will it take the beetle population to reach 200 if it is growing exponentially?

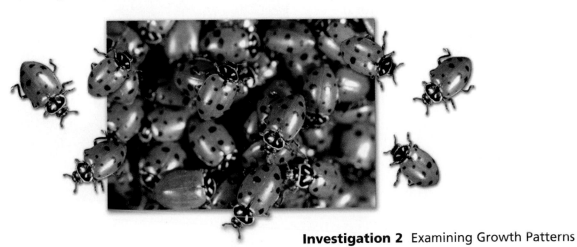

5. Fruit flies are often used in genetic experiments because they reproduce very quickly. In 12 days, a pair of fruit flies can mature and produce a new generation. The table below shows the number of fruit flies in three generations of a laboratory colony.

   a. What is the growth factor for this fruit-fly population? Explain how you found your answer.

Growth of Fruit-Fly Population

Generations	0	1	2	3
Number of Fruit Flies	2	120	7,200	432,000

   b. Suppose this growth pattern continues. How many fruit flies will be in the fifth generation?

   c. Write an equation for the population p of generation g.

   d. After how many generations will the population exceed one billion?

6. A population of mice has a growth factor of 3. After 1 month, there are 36 mice. After 2 months, there are 108 mice.

   a. How many mice were in the population initially (at 0 months)?

   b. Write an equation for the population after any number of months. Explain what information the numbers and variables in your equation represent.

7. Fido did not have fleas when his owners took him to the kennel. The number of fleas on Fido after he returned from the kennel grew according to the equation $f = 8(3^n)$, where f is the number of fleas and n is the number of weeks since he returned from the kennel. (Fido left the kennel at week 0.)

   a. How many fleas did Fido pick up at the kennel?

   b. What is the growth factor for the number of fleas?

   c. How many fleas will Fido have after 10 weeks if he is not treated?

8. Consider the equation $y = 150(2^x)$.

    a. Make a table of x and y-values for whole-number x-values from 0 to 5.

    b. What do the numbers 150 and 2 in the equation tell you about the relationship?

For Exercises 9–12, find the growth factor and the y-intercept of the equation's graph.

    9. $y = 300(3^x)$ **10.** $y = 300(3)^x$

   11. $y = 6{,}500(2)^x$ **12.** $y = 2(7)^x$

┌Go ●nline
           └──PHSchool.com
For: Multiple-Choice Skills
            Practice
Web Code: apa-3254

13. The following graph represents the population growth of a certain kind of lizard.

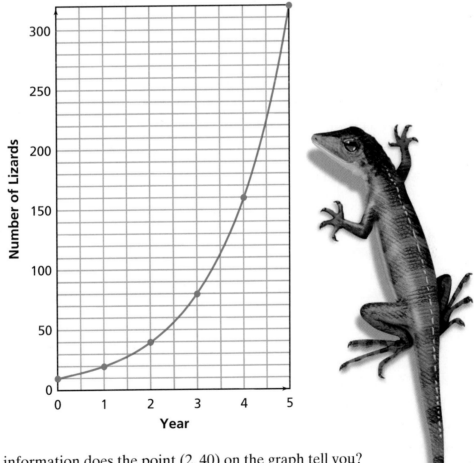

Growth of Lizard Population

    a. What information does the point $(2, 40)$ on the graph tell you?

    b. What information does the point $(1, 20)$ on the graph tell you?

    c. When will the population exceed 100 lizards?

    d. Explain how you can use the graph to find the growth factor for the population.

14. The following graphs show the population growth for two species.

Species X

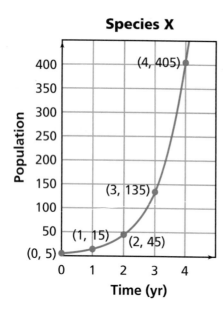

Species Y

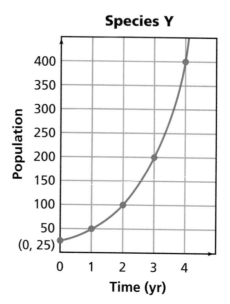

a. Find the growth factors for the two species. Which species is growing faster? Explain.

b. What are the *y*-intercepts for the graphs of Species X and Species Y? Explain what these *y*-intercepts tell you about the populations.

c. Write an equation that describes the growth of Species X.

d. Write an equation that describes the growth of Species Y.

e. For which equation is (5, 1215) a solution?

Connections

15. Multiple Choice Choose the answer that best approximates 3^{20} in scientific notation.

    A. 3.5×10^{-9} **B.** 8×10^{3} **C.** 3×10^{9} **D.** 3.5×10^{9}

16. Multiple Choice Choose the answer that is closest to 2.575×10^{6}.

    F. 2^{18} **G.** 12^{6} **H.** 6^{12} **J.** 11^{9}

17. Approximate 5^{11} in scientific notation.

For Exercises 18–20, decide whether each number is less than or greater than one million *without using a calculator*. Explain your reasoning.

18. 3^{6} **19.** 9^{5} **20.** 12^{6}

21. The prime factorization of 54 is $3 \times 3 \times 3 \times 2$. This can be written using exponents as $3^3 \times 2$. Write the prime factorization of each number using exponents.

a. 45   **b.** 144   **c.** 2,024

22. Consider these equations.

    Equation 1: $y = 10 - 5x$ **Equation 2:** $y = (10)5^x$

a. What is the y-intercept of each equation?

b. For each equation, explain how you could use a table to find how the y-values change as the x-values increase. Describe the change.

c. Explain how you could use the equations to find how the y-values change as the x-values increase.

d. For each equation, explain how you could use a graph to find how the y-values change as the x-values increase.

23. Maria enlarges a 2-cm-by-3-cm rectangle by a factor of 2 to get a 4-cm-by-6-cm rectangle. She then enlarges the 4-cm-by-6-cm rectangle by a factor of 2. She continues this process, enlarging each new rectangle by a factor of 2.

2 cm

3 cm

a. Copy and complete the table to show the dimensions, perimeter, and area of the rectangle after each enlargement.

Rectangle Changes

Enlargement	Dimensions (cm)	Perimeter (cm)	Area (cm²)
0 (original)	2 by 3	■	■
1	4 by 6	■	■
2	■	■	■
3	■	■	■
4	■	■	■
5	■	■	■

b. Is the pattern of growth for the perimeter *linear, exponential,* or *neither*? Explain.

c. Is the pattern of growth for the area *linear, exponential,* or *neither*? Explain.

d. Write an equation for the perimeter P after n enlargements.

e. Write an equation for the area A after n enlargements.

f. How would your answers to parts (a)–(e) change if the copier were set to enlarge by a factor of 3?

Write an equation for each line. Identify the slope and *y*-intercept.

24.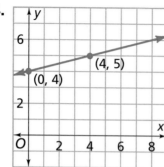

25.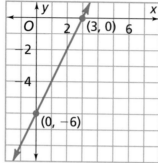

26.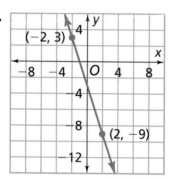

27.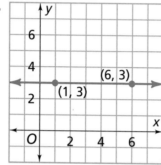

Kele enlarged the figure below by a scale factor of 2. Ahmad enlarged the figure 250%. Use this information for Exercises 28 and 29.

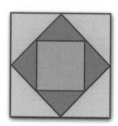

28. Who made the larger image?

29. **Multiple Choice** Which scale factor would give an image whose size is between those of Ahmad's image and Kele's image?

A. $\frac{2}{5}$ **B.** $\frac{3}{5}$ **C.** $\frac{9}{4}$ **D.** $\frac{10}{4}$

30. Companies sometimes describe part-time jobs by comparing them to full-time jobs. For example, a job that requires working half the number of hours of a full-time job is described as a $\frac{1}{2}$-time job or a 50%-time job. ACME, Inc. has three part-time job openings:

- A $\frac{5}{6}$-time job as a gadget inspector

- A 75%-time job as a widget designer

- A 0.875-time job as a gizmo seller

Order these jobs from the one requiring the most time to the one requiring the least time.

Extensions

31. a. Make a table and a graph for the exponential equation $y = 1^x$.

b. How are the patterns in the table and the graph of $y = 1^x$ similar to patterns you have observed for other exponential relationships? How are they different?

32. You can find the equation for an exponential relationship if you know two points on its graph. Find the equation of the exponential relationship whose graph passes through each pair of points. Explain.

a. $(1, 6)$ and $(2, 12)$ **b.** $(2, 90)$ and $(4, 810)$

33. Leaping Leonora from Exercise 3 also considered an offer from another team. They promised her $1 million a year for the next 25 years. The same team offered Dribbling Dawn $1 the first year, $2 the second year, $4 the third year, $8 the fourth year, and so on for 25 years.

a. Suppose Leonora and Dawn had both accepted the offers and played for 20 years. At the end of 20 years, who would have received more money?

b. Tell which player would have received more after 21 years, 22 years, 23 years, and 25 years.

Mathematical Reflections 2

In this investigation, you studied quantities that grew exponentially. You looked at how the values changed from one stage to the next, and you wrote equations to find the value at any stage.

Think about your answers to these questions. Discuss your ideas with other students and your teacher. Then write a summary of your findings in your notebook.

1. **a.** Explain how you can use a table, a graph, and an equation to find the *y*-intercept and growth factor for an exponential relationship.

   b. Explain how you can use the *y*-intercept and growth factor to write an equation for an exponential relationship.

2. **a.** In the equation $y = a(b^x)$, explain what the values of *a* and *b* represent in the exponential relationship.

   b. How is *a* represented in a graph of $y = a(b^x)$?

   c. How is *b* represented in a graph of $y = a(b^x)$?

Investigation 3

Growth Factors and Growth Rates

In the previous investigation, you studied exponential growth of plants, mold, and a snake population. In each case, once you knew the growth factor and the starting value, you could make predictions. The growth factors in these examples were whole numbers. In this investigation, you will study examples of exponential growth with fractional growth factors.

3.1 Reproducing Rabbits

In 1859, a small number of rabbits were introduced to Australia by English settlers. The rabbits had no natural predators in Australia, so they reproduced rapidly and became a serious problem, eating grasses intended for sheep and cattle.

Did You Know?

In the mid-1990s, there were more than 300 million rabbits in Australia. The damage they caused cost Australian agriculture $600 million per year. There have been many attempts to curb Australia's rabbit population. In 1995, a deadly rabbit disease was deliberately spread, reducing the rabbit population by about half. However, because rabbits are developing immunity to the disease, the effects of this measure may not last.

If biologists had counted the rabbits in Australia in the years after they were introduced, they might have collected data like these:

**Growth of
Rabbit Population**

Time (yr)	Population
0	100
1	180
2	325
3	583
4	1,050

A. The table shows the rabbit population growing exponentially.

  1. What is the growth factor? Explain how you found your answer.

  2. Assume this growth pattern continued. Write an equation for the rabbit population p for any year n after the rabbits are first counted. Explain what the numbers in your equation represent.

  3. How many rabbits will there be after 10 years? How many will there be after 25 years? After 50 years?

  4. In how many years will the rabbit population exceed one million?

B. Suppose that, during a different time period, the rabbit population could be predicted by the equation $p = 15(1.2^n)$, where p is the population in millions, and n is the number of years.

  1. What is the growth factor?

  2. What was the initial population?

  3. In how many years will the population double from the initial population?

  4. What will the population be after 3 years? After how many more years will the population at 3 years double?

  5. What will the population be after 10 years? After how many more years will the population at 10 years double?

  6. How do the doubling times for parts (3)–(5) compare? Do you think the doubling time will be the same for this relationship no matter where you start to count?

ACE Homework starts on page 38.

Investing for the Future

The yearly growth factor for one of the rabbit populations in Problem 3.1 is about 1.8. Suppose the population data fit the equation $P = 100(1.8)^n$ exactly. Then its table would look like the one below.

Rabbit Population Growth

n	P
0	100
1	$100 \times 1.8 =$ 180
2	$180 \times 1.8 =$ 324
3	$324 \times 1.8 =$ 583.2
4	$583.2 \times 1.8 =$ 1049.76

The growth factor of 1.8 is the number by which the population for year n is multiplied to get the population for the next year, $n + 1$.

You can think of the growth factor in terms of a percent change. To find the percent change, compare the difference in population for two consecutive years, n and $n + 1$, with the population of year n.

- From year 0 to year 1, the percent change is $\frac{180 - 100}{100} = \frac{80}{100} = 80\%$. The population of 100 rabbits in year 0 *increased* by 80%, resulting in 100 rabbits $\times$ 80% = 80 additional rabbits.

- From year 1 to year 2 the percent change is $\frac{324 - 180}{180} = \frac{144}{180} = 80\%$. The population of 180 rabbits in year 1 *increased* by 80%, resulting in 180 rabbits $\times$ 80% = 144 additional rabbits.

The percent increase is called the **growth rate.** In some growth situations, the growth rate is given instead of the growth factor. For example, changes in the value of investments are often expressed as percents.

Did You Know?

Some investors use a rule of thumb called the "Rule of 72" to approximate how long it will take the value of an investment to double. To use this rule, simply divide 72 by the annual interest rate. For example, an investment at an 8% interest rate will take approximately 72 ÷ 8, or 9, years to double. At a 10% interest rate, the value of an investment will double approximately every 7.2 years. This rule doesn't give you exact doubling times, only approximations.

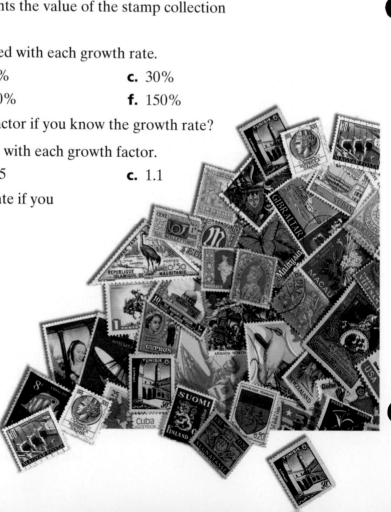

Problem 3.2 Growth Rates

When Sam was in seventh grade, his aunt gave him a stamp collection worth $2,500. Sam considered selling the collection, but his aunt told him that, if he saved it, it would increase in value.

A. Sam saved the collection, and its value increased by 6% each year for several years in a row.

   1. Make a table showing the value of the collection each year for the five years after Sam's aunt gave it to him.

   2. Look at the pattern of growth from one year to the next. Is the value growing exponentially?

   3. Write an equation for the value v of the collection after n years.

B. Suppose the value of the stamps increased by 4% each year instead of by 6%.

   1. Make a table showing the value of the collection each year for the five years after Sam's aunt gave it to him.

   2. What is the growth factor from one year to the next?

   3. Write an equation that represents the value of the stamp collection for any year.

C. 1. Find the growth factor associated with each growth rate.

    a. 5%   **b.** 15%   **c.** 30%

    d. 75%   **e.** 100%   **f.** 150%

   2. How you can find the growth factor if you know the growth rate?

D. 1. Find the growth rate associated with each growth factor.

    a. 1.5   **b.** 1.25   **c.** 1.1

   2. How can you find the growth rate if you know the growth factor?

ACE Homework starts on page 38.

3.3 Making a Difference

In Problem 3.2, the value of Sam's stamp collection increased by the same percent each year. However, each year, this percent was applied to the previous year's value. So, for example, the increase from year 1 to year 2 is 6% of $2,650, not 6% of the original $2,500. This type of change is called **compound growth.**

In the next problem, you will continue to explore compound growth. You will consider the effects of both the initial value and the growth factor on the value of an investment.

Problem 3.3 Connecting Growth Rate and Growth Factor

Cassie's grandmother started college funds for her two granddaughters. She gave $1,250 to Cassie and $2,500 to Cassie's older sister, Kayle. Each fund was invested in a 10-year bond that pays 4% interest a year.

A. For each fund, write an equation to show the relationship between the number of years and the amount of money in the fund.

B. Make a table to show the amount in each fund for 0 to 10 years.

C. 1. How does the initial value of the fund affect the yearly value increases?

    2. How does the initial value affect the growth factor?

    3. How does the initial value affect the final value?

D. A year later, Cassie's grandmother started a fund for Cassie's younger brother, Matt. Cassie made this calculation to predict the value of Matt's fund several years from now:

$$\text{Value} = \$2,000 \times 1.05 \times 1.05 \times 1.05 \times 1.05$$

    1. What initial value, growth rate, growth factor, and number of years is Cassie assuming?

    2. If the value continues to increase at this rate, how much would the fund be worth in one more year?

ACE Homework starts on page 38.

Applications

1. In parts of the United States, wolves are being reintroduced to wilderness areas where they had become extinct. Suppose 20 wolves are released in northern Michigan, and the yearly growth factor for this population is expected to be 1.2.

   a. Make a table showing the projected number of wolves at the end of each of the first 6 years.

   b. Write an equation that models the growth of the wolf population.

   c. How long will it take for the new wolf population to exceed 100?

2. a. The table shows that the elk population in a state forest is growing exponentially. What is the growth factor? Explain.

Growth of Elk Population

Time (yr)	Population
0	30
1	57
2	108
3	206
4	391
5	743

   b. Suppose this growth pattern continues. How many elk will there be after 10 years? How many elk will there be after 15 years?

   c. Write an equation you could use to predict the elk population p for any year n after the elk were first counted.

   d. In how many years will the population exceed one million?

3. Suppose there are 100 trout in a lake and the yearly growth factor for the population is 1.5. How long will it take for the number of trout to double?

4. Suppose there are 500,000 squirrels in a forest and the growth factor for the population is 1.6 per year. Write an equation you could use to find the squirrel population p in n years.

5. **Multiple Choice** The equation $p = 200(1.1)^t$ models the growth of a population. The variable p is the population in millions and t is the time in years. How long will it take this population to double?

A. 4 to 5 years   **B.** 5 to 6 years   **C.** 6 to 7 years   **D.** 7 to 8 years

In Exercises 6 and 7, the equation models the growth of a population, where p is the population in millions and t is the time in years. Tell how much time it would take the population to double.

6. $p = 135(1.7)^t$ **7.** $p = 1,000(1.2)^t$

8. a. Fill in the table for each equation.

$y = 50(2.2)^x$

x	0	1	2	3	4	5
y	▪	▪	▪	▪	▪	▪

$y = 350(1.7)^x$

x	0	1	2	3	4	5
y	▪	▪	▪	▪	▪	▪

b. What is the growth factor for each equation?

c. Predict whether the graphs of these equations will ever cross.

d. Estimate any points at which you think the graphs will cross.

9. Maya's grandfather opened a savings account for her when she was born. He opened the account with $100 and did not add or take out any money after that. The money in the account grows at a rate of 4% per year.

a. Make a table to show the amount in the account from the time Maya was born until she turned 10.

b. What is the growth factor for the account?

c. Write an equation for the value of the account after any number of years.

Homework Help Online
PHSchool.com

For: Help with Exercise 9
Web Code: ape-3309

Find the growth rate associated with the given growth factor.

10. 1.4   **11.** 1.9   **12.** 1.75

Go Online
PHSchool.com

For: Multiple-Choice Skills Practice
Web Code: apa-3354

For Exercises 13–15, find the growth factor associated with the given growth rate.

13. 45%   **14.** 90%   **15.** 31%

16. Suppose the price of an item increases by 25% per year. What is the growth factor for the price from year to year?

17. Currently, 1,000 students attend Greenville Middle School. The school can accommodate 1,300 students. The school board estimates that the student population will grow by 5% per year for the next several years.

  a. In how many years will the population outgrow the present building?

  b. Suppose the school limits its growth to 50 students per year. How many years will it take for the population to outgrow the school?

18. Suppose that, for several years, the number of radios sold in the United States increased by 3% each year.

  a. Suppose one million radios sold in the first year of this time period. About how many radios sold in each of the next 6 years?

  b. Suppose only 100,000 radios sold in the first year. About how many radios sold in each of the next 6 years?

19. Suppose a movie ticket costs about $7, and inflation causes ticket prices to increase by 4.5% a year for the next several years.

  a. At this rate, how much will a ticket cost 5 years from now?

  b. How much will a ticket cost 10 years from now?

  c. How much will a ticket cost 30 years from now?

20. Find the growth rate (percent growth) for a relationship with the equation $y = 30(2^x)$.

21. Multiple Choice Ms. Diaz wants to invest $500 in a savings bond. At which bank would her investment grow the most over 8 years?

   F. Bank 1: 7% interest for 8 years.

   G. Bank 2: 2% interest for the first 4 years and 12% interest for the next four years.

   H. Bank 3: 12% interest for the first 4 years and 2% interest for the next four years.

   J. All three result in the same growth.

22. Oscar made the following calculation to predict the value of his baseball card collection several years from now:

$$\text{Value} = \$130 \times 1.07 \times 1.07 \times 1.07 \times 1.07 \times 1.07$$

   a. What initial value, growth rate, growth factor, and number of years is Oscar assuming?

   b. If the value continues to increase at this rate, how much would the collection be worth in three more years?

23. Carlos, Latanya, and Mila work in a biology laboratory. Each of them is responsible for a population of mice.

   ● The growth factor for Carlos's population of mice is $\frac{8}{7}$.

   ● The growth factor for Latanya's population of mice is 3.

   ● The growth factor for Mila's population of mice is 125%.

   a. Whose mice are reproducing fastest?

   b. Whose mice are reproducing slowest?

Connections

Calculate each percent.

24. 120% of $3,000 **25.** 150% of $200 **26.** 133% of $2,500

For Exercises 27–30, tell whether the sequence of numbers could represent an exponential growth pattern. Explain your reasoning. If the pattern is exponential, give the growth factor.

27. 1 1.1 1.21 1.331 1.4641 1.61051 1.771561

28. 3 5 $8\frac{1}{3}$ $13\frac{8}{9}$ $23\frac{4}{27}$

29. 3 $4\frac{2}{3}$ $6\frac{1}{3}$ 8 $9\frac{2}{3}$ $11\frac{1}{3}$

30. 2 6.4 20.5 66 210

31. The graph shows the growth in the number of wireless subscribers in the United States from 1994 to 2004.

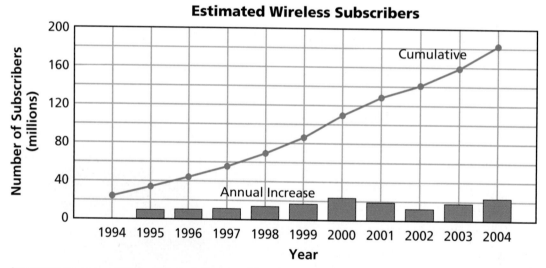

Estimated Wireless Subscribers

SOURCE: CTIA Semi-Annual Wireless Industry Indices, June 2004 Edition. Used with permission of the CTIA-The Wireless Association®

a. What do the bars in the graph represent?

b. What does the curve represent?

c. Describe the pattern of change in the total number of subscribers from 1994 to 2004. Could the pattern be exponential? Explain.

d. The number of subscribers in 2001 was 128,375,000 and in 2002 the number was 140,455,000. Do these numbers fit the pattern you described in part (c)? Explain.

42 Growing, Growing, Growing

32. A worker currently receives a yearly salary of $20,000.

    a. Find the dollar values of a 3%, 4%, and 6% raise for this worker.

    b. Find the worker's new annual salary for each raise in part (a).

    c. You can find the new salary after a 3% raise in two ways:
        $20,000 + 3% of ($20,000) *or* 103% of $20,000

    Explain why these two methods give the same result.

33. Arturo enlarges this drawing to 110% of this size. Make a copy of the drawing on grid paper and use it as you answer the following questions.

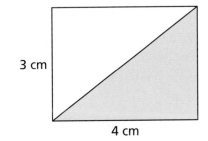

3 cm

4 cm

    a. What is the length of the diagonal in the original drawing? What is the area of the shaded region?

    b. What is the length of the diagonal in the enlarged drawing? What is the area of the shaded region?

    c. Arturo enlarges the enlargement to 110% of its size. He continues this process, enlarging each new drawing to 110% of its size. After five enlargements, what will the length of the diagonal and the area of the shaded region be?

    d. Is each enlargement similar to the original figure? Explain. (**Hint:** Compare the ratio of the length to the width for each enlargement with the ratio of the length to the width for the original.)

34. Kwan cuts lawns every summer to make money. One of her customers offers to give her a 3% raise next summer and a 4% raise the summer after that.

Kwan says she would prefer to get a 4% raise next summer and a 3% raise the summer after that. She claims she will earn more money this way. Is she correct? Explain.

35. After graduating from high school, Kim accepts a job with a package delivery service, earning $9 per hour.

  a. How much will Kim earn in a year if she works 40 hours per week for 50 weeks and gets 2 weeks of paid vacation time?

  b. Write an equation showing the relationship between the number of weeks Kim works w and the amount she earns a.

  c. Kim writes the following equation: $9{,}000 = 360w$. What question is she trying to answer? What is the answer to that question?

  d. Suppose Kim works for the company for 10 years, receiving a 3% raise each year. Make a table showing how her annual income grows over this time period.

  e. When Kim was hired, her manager told her that instead of a 3% annual raise, she could choose to receive a $600 raise each year. How do the two raise plans compare over a 10-year period? Which plan do you think is better? Explain your answer.

36. Which represents faster growth, a growth factor of 2.5 or a growth rate of 25%?

37. Order these scale factors from least to greatest.

130% $\dfrac{3}{2}$ 2   1.475

38. Christopher made a drawing that measures $8\frac{1}{2}$ by 11 inches. He needs to reduce it so it will fit into a space that measures $7\frac{1}{2}$ by 10 inches. What scale factor should he use to get a similar drawing that is small enough to fit? (Do not worry about getting it to fit perfectly.)

39. a. Match each growth rate from List 1 with the equivalent growth factor in List 2 if possible.

  List 1: 20%, 120%, 50%, 200%, 400%, 2%

  List 2: 1.5, 5, 1.2, 2.2, 4, 2, 1.02

  b. Order the growth rates from List 1 from least to greatest.

  c. Order the growth factors from List 2 from least to greatest.

Extensions

40. In Russia, shortly after the breakup of the Soviet Union, the yearly growth factor for inflation was 26. What growth rate (percent increase) is associated with this growth factor? We call this percent increase the *inflation rate*.

41. In 1990, the population of the United States was about 250 million and was growing exponentially at a rate of about 1% per year.

    a. At this growth rate, what will the population of the United States be in the year 2010?

    b. At this rate, how long will it take the population to double?

    c. Do you think the predictions in parts (a) and (b) are accurate? Explain.

    d. The population in 2000 was about 282 million. How accurate was the growth rate?

42. Use the table to answer parts (a)–(d).

    a. One model of world population growth assumes the population grows exponentially. Based on the data in this table, what would be a reasonable growth factor for this model?

    b. Use your growth factor from part (a) to write an equation for the growth of the population at 5-year intervals beginning in 1955.

    c. Use your equation from part (b) to estimate the year in which the population was double the 1955 population.

    d. Use your equation to predict when the population will be double the 2000 population.

World Population Growth

Year	Population (billions)
1955	2.76
1960	3.02
1965	3.33
1970	3.69
1975	4.07
1980	4.43
1985	4.83
1990	5.26
1995	5.67
2000	6.07

Write an exponential growth equation that matches each description.

43. A population is initially 300. After 1 year, the population is 360.

44. A population has a yearly growth factor of 1.2. After 3 years, the population is 1,000.

45. The growth rate for an investment is 3% per year. After 2 years, the value of the investment is $2,560.

46. Suppose your calculator did not have an exponent key. You could find 1.5^{12} by entering:

$1.5 \times 1.5 \times 1.5 \times 1.5 \times 1.5 \times 1.5 \times 1.5 \times 1.5 \times 1.5 \times 1.5 \times 1.5 \times 1.5$

a. How could you evaluate 1.5^{12} with fewer keystrokes?

b. What is the fewest number of times you could press ✕ to evaluate 1.5^{12}?

47. Mr. Watson sold his boat for $10,000. He wants to invest the money.

a. How much money will he have after 1 year if he invests the $10,000 in an account that pays 4% interest per year?

b. Mr. Watson sees an advertisement for another type of savings account:

"4% interest per year compounded quarterly."

He asks the bank teller what "compounded quarterly" means. She explains that instead of giving him 4% of $10,000 at the end of one year, the bank will give him 1% at the end of each 3-month period (each quarter of a year).

Growth of $10,000 Investment at 4% Interest Compounded Quarterly

Time (mo)	Money in Account
0	$10,000
3	$10,100
6	$10,201
9	$10,303.01

If Mr. Watson invests his money at this bank, how much will be in his account at the end of one year?

c. Mr. Watson sees an advertisement for a different bank that offers 4% interest per year *compounded monthly.* (This means he will get $\frac{1}{12}$ of 4% interest every month.) How much money will he have at the end of the year if he invests his money at this bank?

d. Which account would have the most money at the end of one year? Explain.

Mathematical Reflections 3

In this investigation, you explored exponential growth situations in which the growth factor was not a whole number. In some of these situations, the growth was described by giving the percent growth, or growth rate.

Think about your answers to these questions. Discuss your ideas with other students and your teacher. Then write a summary of your findings in your notebook.

1. Suppose you know the initial value for a population and the yearly growth rate.

   a. How can you determine the population several years from now?

   b. How is a growth rate related to the growth factor for the population?

2. Suppose you know the initial value for a population and the yearly growth factor.

   a. How can you determine the population several years from now?

   b. How can you determine the yearly growth rate?

3. Suppose you know the equation that represents the exponential relationship between the population size p and the number of years n. How can you determine the doubling time for the population?

Exponential Decay

The exponential patterns you have studied so far have all involved quantities that increase. In this investigation, you will explore quantities that decrease, or *decay*, exponentially as time passes.

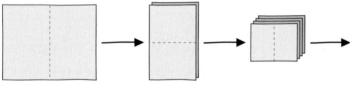

4.1 Making Smaller Ballots

In Problem 1.1, you read about the ballots Chen, the secretary of the Student Government Association, is making for a meeting. Recall that Chen cuts a sheet of paper in half, stacks the two pieces and cuts them in half, stacks the resulting four pieces and cuts them in half, and so on.

You investigated the pattern in the number of ballots created by each cut. In this problem, you will look at the pattern in the areas of the ballots.

BALLOTS

Problem 4.1 Introducing Exponential Decay

A. The paper Chen starts with has an area of 64 square inches. Copy and complete the table to show the area of a ballot after each of the first 10 cuts.

Number of Cuts	Area (in.^{2})
0	64
1	32
2	16
3	■
4	■
5	■
6	■
7	■
8	■
9	■
10	■

B. How does the area of a ballot change with each cut?

C. Write an equation for the area A of a ballot after any cut n.

D. Make a graph of the data.

E. How is the pattern of change in the area different from the exponential growth patterns you studied? How is it similar?

ACE Homework starts on page 53.

4.2 Fighting Fleas

Exponential patterns like the one in Problem 4.1, in which a quantity decreases at each stage, show **exponential decay.** The factor the quantity is multiplied by at each stage is called the **decay factor.** A decay factor is always less than 1 but greater than 0. In Problem 4.1, the decay factor is $\frac{1}{2}$.

After an animal receives a preventive flea medicine, the medicine breaks down in the animal's bloodstream. With each hour, there is less medicine in the blood. The table and graph show the amount of medicine in a dog's bloodstream each hour for 6 hours after receiving a 400-milligram dose.

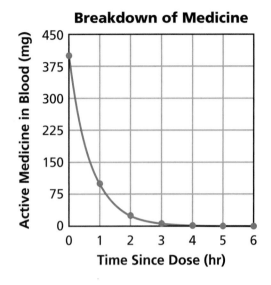

Breakdown of Medicine

Time Since Dose (hr)	Active Medicine in Blood (mg)
0	400
1	100
2	25
3	6.25
4	1.5625
5	0.3907
6	0.0977

Problem 4.2 Representing Exponential Decay

A. Study the pattern of change in the graph and the table.

1. How does the amount of active medicine in the dog's blood change from one hour to the next?

2. Write an equation to model the relationship between the number of hours h since the dose is given and the milligrams of active medicine m.

3. How is the graph for this problem similar to the graph you made in Problem 4.1? How is it different?

B. 1. A different flea medicine breaks down at a rate of 20% per hour. This means that as each hour passes, 20% of the active medicine is used. The initial dose is 60 milligrams. Extend and complete this table to show the amount of active medicine in an animal's blood at the end of each hour for 6 hours.

Breakdown of Medicine

Time Since Dose (hr)	Active Medicine in Blood (mg)
0	60
1	■
2	■
⋮	⋮
6	■

2. For the medicine in part (1), Janelle wrote the equation $m = 60(0.8)^h$ to show the amount of active medicine m after h hours. Compare the quantities of active medicine in your table with the quantities given by Janelle's equation. Explain any similarities or differences.

3. Dwayne was confused by the terms **decay rate** and *decay factor*. He said that because the rate of decay is 20%, the decay factor should be 0.2, and the equation should be $m = 60(0.2^h)$. How would you explain to Dwayne why a rate of decay of 20% is equivalent to a decay factor of 0.8?

ACE Homework starts on page 53.

4.3 Cooling Water

Sometimes a cup of hot cocoa or tea is too hot to drink at first, so you must wait for it to cool.

What pattern of change would you expect to find in the temperature of a hot drink as time passes?

*What shape would you expect for a graph of (*time, drink temperature*) data?*

This experiment will help you explore these questions.

Equipment:

- very hot water, a thermometer, a cup or mug for hot drinks, and a watch or clock

Directions:

- Record the air temperature.
- Fill the cup with the hot water.
- In a table, record the water temperature and the room temperature in 5-minute intervals throughout your class period.

Hot Water Cooling

Time (min)	Water Temperature	Room Temperature
0	▪	▪
5	▪	▪
10	▪	▪
▪	▪	▪
▪	▪	▪

A. 1. Make a graph of your (*time, water temperature*) data.

2. Describe the pattern of change in the data. When did the water temperature change most rapidly? When did it change most slowly?

B. 1. Add a column to your table. In this column, record the difference between the water temperature and the air temperature for each time value.

2. Make a graph of the (*time, temperature difference*) data. Compare this graph with the graph you made in Question A.

3. Describe the pattern of change in the (*time, temperature difference*) data. When did the temperature difference change most rapidly? When did it change most slowly?

4. Estimate the decay factor for the relationship between temperature difference and time in this experiment.

5. Find an equation for the (*time, temperature difference*) data. Your equation should allow you to predict the temperature difference at the end of any 5-minute interval.

C. 1. What do you think the graph of the (*time, temperature difference*) data would look like if you had continued the experiment for several more hours?

2. What factors might affect the rate at which a cup of hot liquid cools?

3. What factors might introduce errors in the data you collect?

D. Compare the two graphs in Questions A and B with the graphs in Problems 4.1 and 4.2. What similarities and differences do you observe?

ACE Homework starts on page 53.

Applications

1. Latisha has a 24-inch string of licorice (LIK uh rish) to share with her friends. As each friend asks her for a piece, Latisha gives him or her half of what she has left. She doesn't eat any of the licorice herself.

   a. Make a table showing the length of licorice Latisha has left each time she gives a piece away.

   b. Make a graph of the data from part (a).

   c. Suppose that, instead of half the licorice that is left each time, Latisha gives each friend 4 inches of licorice. Make a table and a graph for this situation.

   d. Compare the tables and the graphs for the two situations. Explain the similarities and the differences.

2. Chen, from Problem 4.1, finds that his ballots are very small after only a few cuts. He decides to start with a larger sheet of paper. The new paper has an area of 324 in^2. Copy and complete this table to show the area of each ballot after each of the first 10 cuts.

   a. Write an equation for the area A of a ballot after any cut n.

   b. With the smaller sheet of paper, the area of a ballot is 1 in^2 after 6 cuts. How many cuts does it take to get ballots this small, starting with the larger sheet?

   c. Chen wants to be able to make 12 cuts before getting ballots with an area of 1 in^2. How large does his starting piece of paper need to be?

Number of Cuts	Area (in.^{2})
0	324
1	162
2	81
3	■
4	■
5	■
6	■
7	■
8	■
9	■
10	■

3. Penicillin decays exponentially in the human body. Suppose you receive a 300-milligram dose of penicillin to combat strep throat. About 180 milligrams will remain active in your blood after 1 day.

   a. Assume the amount of penicillin active in your blood decreases exponentially. Make a table showing the amount of active penicillin in your blood for 7 days after a 300-milligram dose.

   b. Write an equation for the relationship between the number of days d since you took the penicillin and the amount of the medicine m remaining active in your blood.

   c. What would be the equation if you had taken a 400-milligram dose?

Homework Help Online
PHSchool.com
For: Help with Exercise 3
Web Code: ape-3403

In Exercises 4 and 5, tell whether the equation represents exponential decay or exponential growth. Explain your reasoning.

4. $y = 0.8(2.1)^x$ **5.** $y = 20(0.5)^x$

Go Online
PHSchool.com
For: Multiple-Choice Skills Practice
Web Code: apa-3454

6. The graph below shows an exponential decay relationship.

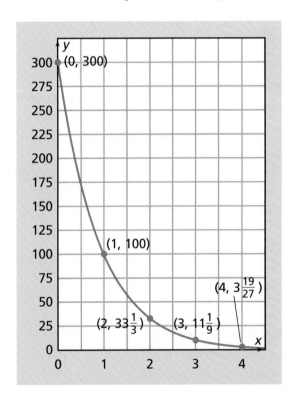

   a. Find the decay factor and the y-intercept.

   b. What is the equation for the graph?

7. Hot coffee is poured into a cup and allowed to cool. The difference between coffee temperature and room temperature is recorded every minute for 10 minutes.

Cooling Coffee

Time (min)	0	1	2	3	4	5	6	7	8	9	10
Temperature Difference (°C)	80	72	65	58	52	47	43	38	34	31	28

a. Plot the (*time, temperature difference*) data. Explain what the patterns in the table and the graph tell you about the rate at which the coffee cools.

b. Approximate the decay factor for this relationship.

c. Write an equation for the relationship between time and temperature difference.

d. About how long will it take the coffee to cool to room temperature? Explain.

Connections

8. Scientific notation is useful for writing very large numbers. Write each of the following numbers in scientific notation.

a. There are about 33,400,000,000,000,000,000,000 molecules in 1 gram of water.

b. There are about 25,000,000,000,000 red blood cells in the human body.

c. Earth is about 93,000,000 miles (150,000,000 km) from the sun.

d. According to the Big Bang Theory, our universe began with an explosion 18,000,000,000 years ago, generating temperatures of 100,000,000,000° Celsius.

9. Consider these equations:

$y = 0.75^x$ $y = 0.25^x$ $y = -0.5x + 1$

a. Sketch graphs of all three equations on one set of axes.

b. What points, if any, do the three graphs have in common?

c. In which graph does y decrease the fastest as x increases?

d. How can you use your graphs to figure out which of the equations is not an example of exponential decay?

e. How can you use the equations to figure out which is not an example of exponential decay?

10. A cricket is on the 0 point of a number line, hopping toward 1. She covers half the distance from her current location to 1 with each hop. So, she will be at $\frac{1}{2}$ after one hop, $\frac{3}{4}$ after two hops, and so on.

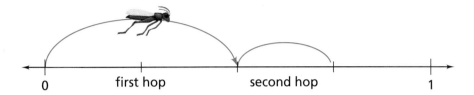

0   first hop   second hop   1

a. Make a table showing the cricket's location for the first 10 hops.

b. Where will the cricket be after n hops?

c. Will the cricket ever get to 1? Explain.

11. The pizza in the ad for Mr. Costa's restaurant has a diameter of 5 inches.

a. What are the circumference and area of the pizza?

b. Mr. Costa reduces his ad to 90% of its original size. He then reduces the reduced ad to 90% of its size. He repeats this process five times. Extend and complete the table to show the diameter, circumference, and area of the pizza after each reduction.

Advertisement Pizza Sizes

Reduction Number	Diameter (in.)	Circumference (in.)	Area (in.²)
0	5	▉	▉
1	▉	▉	▉

c. Write equations for the diameter, circumference, and area of the pizza after n reductions.

d. How would your equations change if Mr. Costa had used a reduction setting of 75%?

e. Express the decay factors from part (d) as fractions.

f. Mr. Costa claims that when he uses the 90% reduction setting on the copier, he is reducing the size of the drawing by 10%. Is Mr. Costa correct? Explain.

12. Answer parts (a) and (b) without using your calculator.

   a. Which decay factor represents faster decay, 0.8 or 0.9?

   b. Order the following from least to greatest:

$$0.9^4 \qquad 0.9^2 \qquad 90\% \qquad \frac{2}{10} \qquad \frac{2}{9} \qquad 0.8^4 \qquad 0.84$$

Extensions

13. Freshly cut lumber, known as *green lumber*, contains water. If green lumber is used to build a house, it may crack, shrink, and warp as it dries. To avoid these problems, lumber is dried in a kiln that circulates air to remove moisture from the wood. Suppose that, in 1 week, a kiln removes $\frac{1}{3}$ of the moisture from a stack of lumber.

   a. What fraction of the moisture remains in the lumber after 5 weeks in a kiln?

   b. What fraction of the moisture has been removed from the lumber after 5 weeks?

   c. Write an equation for the fraction of moisture m remaining in the lumber after w weeks.

   d. Write an equation for the fraction of moisture m that has been removed from the lumber after w weeks.

   e. Graph your equations from parts (c) and (d) on the same set of axes. Describe how the graphs are related.

   f. A different kiln removes $\frac{1}{4}$ of the moisture from a stack of lumber each week. Write equations for the fraction of moisture remaining and the fraction of moisture removed after w weeks.

   g. Graph your two equations from part (f) on the same set of axes. Describe how the graphs are related. How do they compare to the graphs from part (e)?

   h. Green lumber is about 40% water by weight. The moisture content of lumber used to build houses is typically 10% or less. For each of the two kilns described above, how long should lumber be dried before it is used to build a house?

Mathematical Reflections 4

In this investigation, you explored situations that showed patterns of exponential decay.

Think about your answers to these questions. Discuss your ideas with other students and your teacher. Then, write a summary of your findings in your notebook.

1. How can you recognize an exponential decay pattern from a table of data?

2. How can you recognize an exponential decay pattern from a graph?

3. How can you tell that an equation represents exponential decay?

4. How are exponential growth relationships and exponential decay relationships similar? How are they different?

5. How are exponential decay relationships and decreasing linear relationships similar? How are they different?

Patterns With Exponents

As you explored exponential relationships in previous investigations, you made tables of exponential growth. This table shows some values for $y = 2^x$. The y-values are given in both exponential and standard form.

x	y
1	2^1 or 2
2	2^2 or 4
3	2^3 or 8
4	2^4 or 16
5	2^5 or 32
6	2^6 or 64
7	2^7 or 128
8	2^8 or 256

There are many interesting patterns in the table.

Getting Ready for Problem

- Look at the column of y-values in the table. What pattern do you see in how the ones digits of the standard forms change?
- Can you predict the ones digit for 2^{15}? What about 2^{50}?
- What other patterns do you see in the table?
- Find an x-value and values for the missing digits that will make this a true number sentence.

    $2^x = _____6$

5.1 Predicting the Ones Digit

The values of a^x for a given number a are called *powers of a*. You just looked at powers of 2. In this problem, you will explore patterns in other powers.

Problem 5.1 Predicting the Ones Digit

A. Copy and complete this table.

Powers Table

x	1^x	2^x	3^x	4^x	5^x	6^x	7^x	8^x	9^x	10^x
1	1	2								
2	1	4								
3	1	8								
4	1	16								
5	1	32								
6	1	64								
7	1	128								
8	1	256								
Ones Digits of the Powers	1	2, 4, 8, 6								

B. Describe patterns you see in the ones digits of the powers.

C. Predict the ones digit in the standard form of each number.

  1. 4^{12} **2.** 9^{20} **3.** 3^{17} **4.** 5^{100} **5.** 10^{500}

D. Predict the ones digit in the standard form of each number.

  1. 31^{10} **2.** 12^{10} **3.** 17^{21} **4.** 29^{10}

E. Find the value of a that makes each number sentence true.

1. $a^{12} = 531,441$ **2.** $a^9 = 387,420,489$ **3.** $a^6 = 11,390,625$

F. Find a value for a and values for the missing digits to make each number sentence true. Explain your reasoning.

1. $a^7 = $ __ __ __ __ __ 3 **2.** $a^8 = $ __ __ __ __ __ __ __ 1

ACE Homework starts on page 64.

5.2 Operating With Exponents

In the last problem, you explored patterns in the values of a^x for different values of a. You used the patterns you discovered to make predictions. For example, you predicted the ones digit in the standard form of 4^{12}. In this problem, you will look at other interesting patterns that lead to some important properties of exponents.

Getting Ready for Problem 5.2

- Federico noticed that 16 appears twice in the powers table. It is in the column for 2^x, for $x = 4$. It is also in the column for 4^x, for $x = 2$. He said this means that $2^4 = 4^2$. Write 2^4 as a product of 2's. Then, show that the product is equal to 4^2.

- Are there other numbers that appear more than once in the table? If so, write equations to show the equivalent exponential forms of the numbers.

Use properties of real numbers and your table from Problem 5.1 to help you answer these questions.

A. 1. Explain why each of the following statements is true.

   a. $2^3 \times 2^2 = 2^5$ **b.** $3^4 \times 3^3 = 3^7$ **c.** $6^3 \times 6^5 = 6^8$

2. Give another example that fits the pattern in part (1).

3. Complete the following equation to show how you can find the exponent of the product when you multiply two powers with the same base. Explain your reasoning.

$$a^m \times a^n = a^{\blacksquare}$$

B. 1. Explain why each of the following statements is true.

   a. $2^3 \times 3^3 = 6^3$ **b.** $5^3 \times 6^3 = 30^3$ **c.** $10^4 \times 4^4 = 40^4$

2. Give another example that fits the pattern in part (1).

3. Complete the following equation to show how you can find the base and exponent of the product when you multiply two powers with the same exponent. Explain your reasoning.

$$a^m \times b^m = \underline{\ ?\ }$$

C. 1. Explain why each of the following statements is true.

   a. $4^2 = (2^2)^2 = 2^4$
   b. $9^2 = (3^2)^2 = 3^4$
   c. $125^2 = (5^3)^2 = 5^6$

2. Give another example that fits the pattern in part (1).

3. Complete the following equation to show how you can find the base and exponent when a power is raised to a power. Explain.

$$(a^m)^n = \underline{\ ?\ }$$

D. 1. Explain why each of the following statements is true.

   a. $\dfrac{3^5}{3^2} = 3^3$ **b.** $\dfrac{4^6}{4^5} = 4^1$ **c.** $\dfrac{5^{10}}{5^{10}} = 5^0$

2. Tom says $\dfrac{4^5}{4^6} = 4^{-1}$. Mary says $\dfrac{4^5}{4^6} = \dfrac{1}{4^1}$. Who is correct and why?

3. Complete the following equation to show how you can find the base and exponent of the quotient when you divide two powers with the same base. (Assume a is not 0.) Explain your reasoning.

$$\frac{a^m}{a^n} = \underline{\ ?\ }$$

E. Use the pattern from Question D to explain why $a^0 = 1$ for any nonzero number a.

ACE Homework starts on page 64.

5.3 Exploring Exponential Equations

In this unit, you have studied situations that show patterns of exponential growth or exponential decay. All of these situations are modeled by equations of the form $y = a(b^x)$, where a is the starting value and b is the growth or decay factor.

Problem 5.3 Exploring Exponential Equations

You can use your graphing calculator to explore how the values of a and b affect the graph of $y = a(b^x)$.

A. First, let $a = 1$ and explore how the value of b affects the graph of $y = b^x$.

   1. Graph these four equations in the same window. Use window settings that show x-values from -5 to 5 and y-values from -5 to 20. Record your observations.

      $y = 1.25^x$ $y = 1.5^x$ $y = 1.75^x$ $y = 2^x$

   2. Next, graph these three equations in the same window. Use window settings that show $-5 \leq x \leq 5$ and $-1 \leq y \leq 2$. Record your observations.

      $y = 0.25^x$ $y = 0.5^x$ $y = 0.75^x$

   3. Describe how you could predict the general shape of the graph of $y = b^x$ for a specific value of b.

B. Next, you will look at how the value of a affects the graph of $y = a(b^x)$. You will need to adjust the window settings as you work. Graph each set of equations in the same window. Record your observations for each set.

   1. $y = 2(2^x)$ $y = 3(2^x)$ $y = 4(2^x)$

   2. $y = 2(1.5^x)$ $y = 3(1.5^x)$ $y = 4(1.5^x)$

   3. $y = 2(0.5^x)$ $y = 3(0.5^x)$ $y = 4(0.5^x)$

   4. Describe how the value of a affects the graph of an equation of the form $y = a(b^x)$.

ACE Homework starts on page 64.

Applications

Connections

Extensions

ACE

Applications

Predict the ones digit for the standard form of the number.

1. 7^{100} **2.** 6^{200} **3.** 17^{100} **4.** 31^{10} **5.** 12^{100}

active math online
For: Pattern Iterator
Visit: PHSchool.com
Web Code: apd-3500

For Exercises 6 and 7, find the value of a that makes the number sentence true.

6. $a^7 = 823{,}543$ **7.** $a^6 = 1{,}771{,}561$

8. Explain how you can use your calculator to find the ones digit of the standard form of 3^{30}.

9. **Multiple Choice** In the powers table you completed in Problem 5.1, look for patterns in the ones digit of square numbers. Which number is *not* a square number? Explain.

A. 289   **B.** 784   **C.** 1,392   **D.** 10,000

Tell how many zeros are in the standard form of the number.

10. 10^{10} **11.** 10^{50} **12.** 10^{100}

Find the least value of x that will make the statement true.

13. $9^6 < 10^x$ **14.** $3^{14} < 10^x$

For Exercises 15–17, identify the greater number in each pair.

15. 6^{10} or 7^{10} **16.** 8^{10} or 10^8 **17.** 6^9 or 9^6

18. **Multiple Choice** Which expression is equivalent to $2^9 \times 2^{10}$?

F. 2^{90} **G.** 2^{19} **H.** 4^{19} **J.** 2^{18}

Use the properties of exponents to write each expression as a single power. Check your answers.

19. $5^6 \times 8^6$ **20.** $(7^5)^3$ **21.** $\dfrac{8^{15}}{8^{10}}$

64   Growing, Growing, Growing

For Exercises 22–27, tell whether the statement is *true* or *false*. Explain.

Go Online
PHSchool.com
For: Multiple-Choice Skills Practice
Web Code: apa-3554

22. $6^3 \times 6^5 = 6^8$

23. $2^3 \times 3^2 = 6^5$

24. $3^8 = 9^4$

25. $4^3 + 5^3 = 9^3$

26. $2^3 + 2^5 = 2^3(1 + 2^2)$

27. $\dfrac{5^{12}}{5^4} = 5^3$

28. Multiple Choice Which number is the ones digit of $2^{10} \times 3^{10}$?

    A. 2   **B.** 4   **C.** 6   **D.** 8

For Exercises 29 and 30, find the ones digit of the product.

29. $4^{15} \times 3^{15}$

30. $7^{15} \times 4^{20}$

31. Manuela said it must be true that $2^{10} = 2^4 \cdot 2^6$ because she can group $2 \cdot 2 \cdot 2 \cdot 2 \cdot 2 \cdot 2 \cdot 2 \cdot 2 \cdot 2 \cdot 2$ as $(2 \cdot 2 \cdot 2 \cdot 2) \cdot (2 \cdot 2 \cdot 2 \cdot 2 \cdot 2 \cdot 2)$.

$2 \cdot 2 \cdot 2 \cdot 2 = 2^4$

  a. Verify that Manuela is correct by evaluating both sides of the equation $2^{10} = 2^4 \cdot 2^6$.

  b. Use Manuela's idea of grouping factors to write three other expressions that are equivalent to 2^{10}. Evaluate each expression you find to verify that it is equivalent to 2^{10}.

  c. The standard form for 2^7 is 128, and the standard form for 2^5 is 32. Use these facts to evaluate 2^{12}. Explain your work.

  d. Test Manuela's idea to see if it works for exponential expressions with other bases, such as 3^8 or $(1.5)^{11}$. Test several cases. Give an argument supporting your conclusion.

Tell whether the expression is equivalent to 1.25^{10}. Explain your reasoning.

32. $(1.25)^5 \cdot (1.25)^5$

33. $(1.25)^3 \times (1.25)^7$

34. $(1.25) \times 10$

35. $(1.25) + 10$

36. $(1.25^5)^2$

37. $(1.25)^5 \cdot (1.25)^2$

For Exercises 38–41, tell whether the expression is equivalent to $(1.5)^7$. Explain your reasoning.

38. $1.5^5 \times 1.5^2$

39. $1.5^3 \times 1.5^4$

40. 1.5×7

41. $(1.5) + 7$

42. Without actually graphing these equations, describe and compare their graphs. Be as specific as you can.

$y = 4^x$ $y = 0.25^x$ $y = 10(4^x)$ $y = 10(0.25^x)$

Homework Help Online
PHSchool.com
For: Help with Exercise 42
Web Code: ape-3542

43. Each graph below represents an exponential equation of the form $y = ab^x$.

  a. For which of the three functions is the value of a greatest?

  b. For which of the three functions is the value of b greatest?

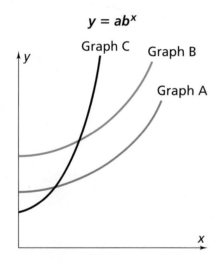

$y = ab^x$

Graph C   Graph B

Graph A

Connections

For Exercises 44 and 45, tell whether the statement is *true* or *false*. Do not do an exact calculation. Explain your reasoning.

44. $(1.56892 \times 10^5) - (2.3456 \times 10^4) < 0$

45. $\dfrac{3.96395 \times 10^5}{2.888211 \times 10^7} > 1$

46. Suppose you start with a unit cube (a cube with edges of length 1 unit). In parts (a)–(c), give the volume and surface area of the cube that results from the given transformation.

   a. Each edge length is doubled.

   b. Each edge length is tripled.

   c. Each edge is enlarged by a scale factor of 100.

47. Suppose you start with a cylinder with a radius of 1 unit and a height of 1 unit. In parts (a)–(c), give the volume of the cylinder that results from the given transformation.

   a. The radius and height are doubled.

   b. The radius and height are tripled.

   c. The radius and height are enlarged by a scale factor of 100.

48. a. Tell which of the following numbers are prime. (There may be more than one.)

   $2^2 - 1 \qquad 2^3 - 1 \qquad 2^4 - 1 \qquad 2^5 - 1 \qquad 2^6 - 1$

   b. Find another prime number that can be written in the form $2^n - 1$.

49. In parts (a)–(d), find the sum of the proper factors for the number.

   a. 2^2 **b.** 2^3 **c.** 2^4 **d.** 2^5

   e. What do you notice about the sums in parts (a)–(d)?

50. Grandville has a population of 1,000. Its population is expected to decrease by 4% a year for the next several years. Tinytown has a population of 100. Its population is expected to increase by 4% a year for the next several years. Will the populations of the two towns ever be the same? Explain.

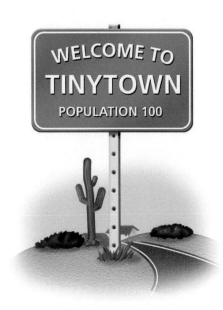

51. The expression $\frac{20}{10^2}$ can be written in equivalent forms, including $\frac{2}{10}$, $\frac{1}{5}$, 0.2, and $\frac{2(10^2)}{10^3}$. In parts (a) and (b), write two equivalent forms for the expression.

a. $\dfrac{3(10)^5}{10^7}$

b. $\dfrac{5(10)^5}{2.5(10)^7}$

Extensions

52. a. Find the sum for each row.

Row 1: $\frac{1}{2}$

Row 2: $\frac{1}{2} + \left(\frac{1}{2}\right)^2$

Row 3: $\frac{1}{2} + \left(\frac{1}{2}\right)^2 + \left(\frac{1}{2}\right)^3$

Row 4: $\frac{1}{2} + \left(\frac{1}{2}\right)^2 + \left(\frac{1}{2}\right)^3 + \left(\frac{1}{2}\right)^4$

b. Study the pattern. Suppose the pattern continues. Write the expression that would be in row 5, and find its sum.

c. What would be the sum of the expression in row 10? What would be the sum for row 20?

d. Describe the pattern of sums in words and with a symbolic expression.

e. For which row does the sum first exceed 0.9?

f. As the row number increases, the sum gets closer and closer to what number?

g. Celeste claims the pattern is related to the pattern of the areas of the ballots cut in Problem 4.1. She drew this picture to explain her thinking. What relationship do you think she has observed?

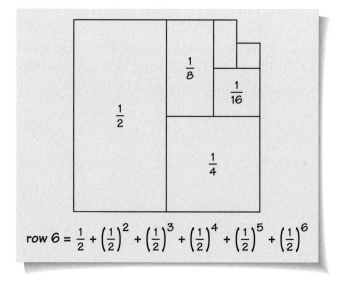

$\text{row } 6 = \frac{1}{2} + \left(\frac{1}{2}\right)^2 + \left(\frac{1}{2}\right)^3 + \left(\frac{1}{2}\right)^4 + \left(\frac{1}{2}\right)^5 + \left(\frac{1}{2}\right)^6$

53. a. Find the sum for each row.

Row 1: $\frac{1}{3}$

Row 2: $\frac{1}{3} + \left(\frac{1}{3}\right)^2$

Row 3: $\frac{1}{3} + \left(\frac{1}{3}\right)^2 + \left(\frac{1}{3}\right)^3$

Row 4: $\frac{1}{3} + \left(\frac{1}{3}\right)^2 + \left(\frac{1}{3}\right)^3 + \left(\frac{1}{3}\right)^4$

b. Study the pattern. Suppose the pattern continues. Write the expression that would be in row 5, and find its sum.

c. What would be the sum of the expression in row 10? What would be the sum for row 20?

d. Describe the pattern of sums in words and with an equation.

e. As the row number increases, the sum gets closer and closer to what number?

54. Negative numbers can be used as exponents. Parts (a) and (b) will help you understand negative exponents.

a. Use your calculator to find the value of 2^x for x-values -1, -2, and -3.

b. Use your calculator to find the value of $\left(\frac{1}{2}\right)^x$ for x-values $1, 2$, and 3.

c. What observation can you make from your computations in parts (a) and (b)?

d. Write each number as a power with a positive exponent.

3^{-1} $\qquad\qquad$ 4^{-2} $\qquad\qquad\qquad$ 5^{-3}

55. a. Copy and complete this table.

Standard Form	Exponential Form
10,000	10^4
1,000	10^3
100	10^2
10	10^1
1	10^0
$\frac{1}{10} = 0.1$	10^{-1}
$\frac{1}{100} = 0.01$	10^{-2}
$\frac{1}{1,000} = 0.001$	▦
$\frac{1}{10,000} = 0.0001$	▦
▦	10^{-5}
▦	10^{-6}

b. Write each number in standard form as a decimal.

$$3 \times 10^{-1} \qquad 1.5 \times 10^{-2} \qquad 1.5 \times 10^{-3}$$

56. If you use your calculator to compute $2 \div 2^{12}$, the display will probably show one of the following:

$$\text{4.8828125E } ^-4 \qquad \text{or} \qquad \text{4.8828125 } _-4$$

Both displays mean 4.8828125×10^{-4}. This number is in scientific notation because it is a number greater than or equal to 1, but less than 10 (in this case, 4.8828125), times a power of 10 (in this case, 10^{-4}). You can convert 4.8828125×10^{-4} to standard form as shown:

$$4.8828125 \times 10^{-4} = 4.8828125 \times \frac{1}{10,000} = 0.00048828125$$

a. Write each number in standard notation.

$$1.2 \times 10^{-1} \qquad 1.2 \times 10^{-2} \qquad 1.2 \times 10^{-3} \qquad 1.2 \times 10^{-8}$$

b. Using what you discovered in part (a), explain how you would write 1.2×10^{-n} in standard notation where n is any whole number greater than or equal to 1.

c. Write each number in scientific notation.

2,000,000   28,000,000   19,900,000,000

0.12489   0.0058421998   0.0010201

57. When Tia found $0.0000015 \div 1,000,000$ on her calculator, she got
1.5E ‾12, which means 1.5×10^{-12}.

   a. Write a different division problem that will give the result 1.5E ‾12
on your calculator.

   b. Write a multiplication problem that will give the result 1.5E ‾12 on
your calculator.

58. The average radius of the moon is
1.74×10^6 meters.

   a. Express the average radius of the
moon in standard notation.

   b. The largest circle that will fit on
this page has a radius of 10.795 cm.
Express this radius in meters,
using scientific notation.

   c. Suppose a circle has the same
radius as the moon. By what scale
factor would the circle have to be
reduced to fit on this page?

59. The number 2^7 is written in standard form as 128 and in scientific
notation as 1.28×10^2. The number $\left(\frac{1}{2}\right)^7$ is written in standard form as
0.0078125 and in scientific notation as 7.812×10^{-3}. Write each
number in scientific notation.

   a. 2^8 **b.** $\left(\frac{1}{2}\right)^8$ **c.** 20^8 **d.** $\left(\frac{1}{20}\right)^8$

60. a. The y-values in the table below are decreasing by a factor of $\frac{1}{3}$.
Copy and complete the table.

x	0	1	2	3	4	5	6	7	8
y	30	10	■	■	■	■	■	■	■

   b. Using a calculator to find the y-value when x is 12 gives the result
5.645029269E ‾5. What does this mean?

   c. Write the y-values for $x = 8, 9, 10,$ and 11 in scientific notation.

61. Chen, from Problem 4.1, decides to make his ballots starting with a sheet of paper with an area of 1 square foot.

a. Copy and complete this table to show the area of each ballot after each of the first 8 cuts.

b. Write an equation for the area A of a ballot after any cut n.

c. Use your equation to find the area of a ballot after 20 cuts. Write your answer in scientific notation.

Number of Cuts	Area (ft²)
0	1
1	$\frac{1}{2}$
2	$\frac{1}{4}$
3	■
4	■
5	■
6	■
7	■
8	■

62. In 1803, the U.S. bought the 828,000-square-mile Louisiana Purchase for $15,000,000. Suppose one of your ancestors was given 1 acre of the Louisiana Purchase. Assuming an annual inflation rate of 4%, what is the value of this acre in 2006? (640 acres = 1 square mile)

63. Use the properties of exponents to show that each statement is true.

a. $\frac{1}{2}(2^n) = 2^{n-1}$ b. $4^{n-1} = \frac{1}{4}(4)^n$ c. $25(5^{n-2}) = 5^n$

Mathematical Reflections 5

In this investigation, you explored properties of exponents and you looked at how the values of a and b affect the graph of $y = a(b^x)$.

Think about your answers to these questions. Discuss your ideas with other students and your teacher. Then, write a summary of your findings in your notebook.

1. Describe some of the rules for operating with exponents.

2. Assume a is a fixed positive number. Describe the graph of $y = a(b^x)$ if

   a. b is greater than 1.

   b. b is equal to 1.

   c. b is between 0 and 1.

3. Assume b is a fixed number greater than 1. Describe the graph of $y = a(b^x)$ if

   a. a is greater than 1.

   b. a is equal to 1.

   c. a is between 0 and 1.

Unit Project

Half-Life

Most things around you are composed of atoms that are stable. However, the atoms that make up *radioactive* substances are unstable—they break down in a process known as *radioactive decay*. As these substances decay, they emit radiation. At high levels, radiation can be dangerous.

The rate of decay varies from substance to substance. The term *half-life* describes the time it takes for half of the atoms in a radioactive sample to decay. For example, the half-life of carbon-11 is 20 minutes. This means that 2,000 carbon-11 atoms will be reduced to 1,000 carbon-11 atoms in 20 minutes, and to 500 carbon-11 atoms in 40 minutes.

Half-lives vary from a fraction of a second to billions of years. For example, the half-life of polonium-214 is 0.00016 seconds. The half-life of rubidium-87 is 49 billion years.

In this experiment, you will model the decay of a radioactive substance known as iodine-124. About $\frac{1}{6}$ of the atoms in a sample of iodine-124 decay each day. This experiment will help you determine the half-life of this substance.

Follow these steps to conduct your experiment:

- Use 100 cubes to represent 100 iodine-124 atoms. Mark one face of each cube.

- Place all 100 cubes in a container, shake the container, and pour the cubes onto the table.

- The cubes for which the mark is facing up represent atoms that have decayed on the first day. Remove these cubes, and record the number of cubes that remain. Place the remaining cubes in the container.

- Repeat this process to find the number of atoms that remain after the second day.

- Repeat this process until one cube or no cubes remain.

When you complete your experiment, answer the questions on the next page.

1. **a.** In your experiment, how many days did it take to reduce the 100 iodine-124 atoms to 50 atoms? In other words, how many times did you have to roll the cubes until about 50 cubes remained?

   b. How many days did it take to reduce 50 iodine-124 atoms to 25 atoms?

   c. Based on your answers to parts (a) and (b), what do you think the half-life of iodine-124 is?

2. **a.** In a sample of real iodine-124, $\frac{1}{6}$ of the atoms decay after 1 day. What fraction of the atoms remain after 1 day?

   b. Suppose a sample contains 100 iodine-124 atoms. Use your answer from part (a) to write an equation for the number of atoms n remaining in the sample after d days.

   c. Use your equation to find the half-life of iodine-124.

   d. How does the half-life you found based on your equation compare to the half-life you found from your experiment?

3. **a.** Make up a problem involving a radioactive substance with a different rate of decay that can be modeled by an experiment involving cubes or other common objects. Describe the situation and your experiment.

   b. Conduct your experiment and record your results.

   c. Use the results of your experiment to predict the half-life of your substance.

   d. Use what you know about the rate of decay to write an equation that models the decay of your substance.

   e. Use your equation to find the half-life of your substance.

Write a report summarizing your findings about decay rates and half-lives. Your report should include tables and graphs justifying your answers to the questions above.

Looking Back and Looking Ahead

Working on the problems in this unit developed your skills in recognizing and applying *exponential relationships* between variables.

Go Online
PHSchool.com
For: Vocabulary Review Puzzle
Web Code: apj-3051

You wrote equations of the form $y = a(b^x)$ to describe *exponential growth* of populations and investments and *exponential decay* of medicines and radioactive materials. You used equations to produce tables and graphs of the relationships. You used those tables and graphs to make predictions and solve equations.

Use Your Understanding: Algebraic Reasoning

To test your understanding and skill in finding and applying exponential models, solve these problems that arise as the student council at Lincoln Middle School plans a fundraising event.

The students want to have a quiz show called *Who Wants to Be Rich?* Contestants will be asked a series of questions. A contestant will play until he or she misses a question. The total prize money will grow with each question answered correctly.

1. Lucy proposes that a contestant receive $5 for answering the first question correctly. For each additional correct answer, the total prize would increase by $10.

   a. For Lucy's proposal, what equation gives the total prize p for correctly answering n questions?

   b. How many questions would a contestant need to answer correctly to win at least $50? To win at least $75? To win at least $100?

   c. Sketch a graph of the (n, p) data for $n = 1$ to 10.

2. Pedro also thinks the first question should be worth $5. However, he thinks a contestant's winnings should double with each subsequent correct answer.

   a. For Pedro's proposal, what equation gives the total prize p for correctly answering n questions?

   b. How many questions will a contestant need to answer correctly to win at least $50? To win at least $75? To win at least $100?

   c. Sketch a graph of the (n, p) data for $n = 1$ to 10.

   d. Compare Pedro's proposal with Lucy's proposal in Exercise 1.

3. The council decides that contestants for *Who Wants to Be Rich?* will be chosen by a random drawing. Students and guests at the fundraiser will buy tickets like the one at right. The purchaser will keep half of the ticket and add the other half to the entries for the drawing.

   a. To make the tickets, council members will take a large piece of paper and fold it in half many times to make a grid of small rectangles. How many rectangles will there be after n folds?

   b. The initial piece of paper will be a square with sides measuring 60 centimeters. What will be the area of each rectangle after n folds?

Decide whether each statement is *true* or *false*. Explain.

4. $3^5 \times 6^5 = 9^5$ **5.** $8^5 \times 4^6 = 2^{27}$ **6.** $\dfrac{20 \times 6^7}{3^7} = 2^7$

Explain Your Reasoning

To answer Questions 1–3, you had to use algebraic knowledge about number patterns, graphs, and equations. You had to recognize linear and exponential patterns from verbal descriptions and represent those patterns with equations and graphs.

7. How can you decide whether a data pattern can be modeled by an exponential equation of the form $y = a(b^x)$? How will the values of a and b relate to the data pattern?

8. Describe the possible shapes for graphs of exponential relationships. How can the shape of an exponential graph be predicted from the values of a and b in the equation?

9. How are the data patterns, graphs, and equations for exponential relationships similar to and different from those for linear relationships?

10. Describe the rules for exponents that you used in Questions 4–6. Choose one of the rules and explain why it works.

Look Ahead

The algebraic ideas and techniques you developed and used in this unit will be applied and extended in future units of *Connected Mathematics* and in problems of science and business. In upcoming units, you will study other important families of algebraic models and you will learn strategies for finding and using those models to solve problems.

English / Spanish Glossary

B

base The number that is raised to a power in an exponential expression. In the expression 3^5, read "3 to the fifth power", 5 is the exponent and 3 is the base.

base El número que se eleva a una potencia en una expresión exponencial. En la expresión 3^5, que se lee "3 elevado a la quinta potencia", 3 es la base y 5 es el exponente.

C

compound growth Another term for exponential growth, usually used when talking about the monetary value of an investment. The change in the balance of a savings account shows compound growth because the bank pays interest not only on the original investment, but on the interest earned.

crecimiento compuesto Otro término para crecimiento exponencial, normalmente usado para referirse al valor monetario de una inversión. El cambio en el saldo de una cuenta de ahorros muestra un crecimiento compuesto, ya que el banco paga intereses no sólo sobre la inversión original, sino sobre los intereses ganados.

D

decay factor The constant factor that each value in an exponential decay pattern is multiplied by to get the next value. The decay factor is the base in an exponential decay equation. For example, in the equation $A = 64(0.5)n$, where A is the area of a ballot and n is the number of cuts, the decay factor is 0.5. It indicates that the area of a ballot after any number of cuts is 0.5 times the area after the previous number of cuts. In a table of (x, y) values for an exponential decay relationship (with x-values increasing by 1), the decay factor is the ratio of any y-value to the previous y-value.

factor de disminución El factor constante por el cual se multiplica cada valor en un patrón de disminución exponencial para obtener el valor siguiente. El factor de disminución es la base en una ecuación de disminución exponencial. Por ejemplo, en la ecuación $A = 64(0.5)n$, donde A es el área de una papeleta y n es el número de cortes, el factor de disminución es 0.5. Esto indica que el área de una papeleta después de un número cualquiera de cortes es 0.5 veces el área después del número anterior de cortes. En una tabla de valores (x, y) para una relación de disminución exponencial (donde el valor x crece de a 1), el factor de disminución es la razón entre cualquier valor de y y su valor anterior.

decay rate The percent decrease in an exponential decay pattern. A discount, expressed as a percent, is a decay rate. In general, for an exponential pattern with decay factor b, the decay rate is $1 - b$.

tasa de disminución El porcentaje de reducción en un patrón de disminución exponencial. Un descuento, expresado como porcentaje, es una tasa de disminución. En general, para un patrón exponencial con factor de disminución b, la tasa de disminución es $1 - b$.

exponent A number that indicates how many times another number (the base) is to be used as a factor. Exponents are written as raised numbers to the right of the base. In the expression 3^5, read "3 to the fifth power", 5 is the exponent and 3 is the base, so 3^5 means $3 \cdot 3 \cdot 3 \cdot 3 \cdot 3$. In the formula for the area of a square, $A = s^2$, the 2 is an exponent. This formula can also be written as $A = s \cdot s$.

exponente Es un número que indica la cantidad de veces que otro número (la base) se va a usar como factor. Los exponentes se escriben como números elevados a la derecha de la base. En la expresión 3^5, que se lee como "3 elevado a la quinta potencia", 5 es el exponente y 3 es la base. Así, 3^5 significa $3 \cdot 3 \cdot 3 \cdot 3 \cdot 3$. En la fórmula para calcular el área de un cuadrado, $A = s^2$, el 2 es un exponente. Esta fórmula también se puede escribir como $A = s \cdot s$.

exponential decay A pattern of decrease in which each value is found by multiplying the previous value by a constant factor greater than 0 and less than 1. For example, the pattern $27, 9, 3, 1, \frac{1}{3}, \frac{1}{9}, \ldots$ shows exponential decay in which each value is $\frac{1}{3}$ times the previous value.

disminución exponencial Un patrón de disminución en el cual cada valor se calcula multiplicando el valor anterior por un factor constante mayor que 0 y menor que 1. Por ejemplo, el patrón $27, 9, 3, 1, \frac{1}{3}, \frac{1}{9}, \ldots$ muestra una disminución exponencial en la que cada valor es $\frac{1}{3}$ del valor anterior.

exponential form A quantity expressed as a number raised to a power. In exponential form, 32 can be written as 2^5.

forma exponencial Una cantidad que se expresa como un número elevado a una potencia. En forma exponencial, 32 puede escribirse como 2^5.

exponential growth A pattern of increase in which each value is found by multiplying the previous value by a constant factor greater than 1. For example, the doubling pattern $1, 2, 4, 8, 16, 32, \ldots$ shows exponential growth in which each value is 2 times the previous value.

crecimiento exponencial Un patrón de crecimiento en el cual cada valor se calcula multiplicando el valor anterior por un factor constante mayor que 1. Por ejemplo, el patrón $1, 2, 4, 8, 16, 32, \ldots$ muestra un crecimiento exponencial en el que cada valor es el doble del valor anterior.

exponential relationship A relationship that shows exponential growth or decay.

relación exponencial Una relación que muestra crecimiento o disminución exponencial.

growth factor The constant factor that each value in an exponential growth pattern is multiplied by to get the next value. The growth factor is the base in an exponential growth equation. For example, in the equation $A = 25(3)^d$, where A is the area of a patch of mold and d is the number of days, the growth factor is 3. It indicates that the area of the mold for any day is 3 times the area for the previous day. In a table of (x, y) values for an exponential growth relationship (with x-values increasing by 1), the growth factor is the ratio of any y-value to the previous y-value.

factor de crecimiento El factor constante por el cual se multiplica cada valor en un patrón de crecimiento exponencial para obtener el valor siguiente. El factor de crecimiento es la base en una ecuación de crecimiento exponencial. Por ejemplo, en la ecuación $A = 25(3)^d$, donde A es el área enmohecida y d es el número de días, el factor de crecimiento es 3. Esto indica que el área enmohecida en un día cualquiera es 3 veces el área del día anterior. En una tabla de valores (x, y) para una relación de crecimiento exponencial (donde el valor de x aumenta de a 1), el factor exponencial es la razón entre cualquier valor de y y su valor anterior.

growth rate The percent increase in an exponential growth pattern. For example, in Problem 3.1, the number of rabbits increased from 100 to 180 from year 0 to year 1, an 80% increase. From year 1 to year 2, the number of rabbits increased from 180 to 324, an 80% increase. The growth rate for this rabbit population is 80%. Interest, expressed as a percent, is a growth rate. For an exponential growth pattern with a growth factor of b, the growth rate is $b - 1$.

tasa de crecimiento El porcentaje de crecimiento en un patrón de crecimiento exponencial. Por ejemplo, en el Problema 3.1, el número de conejos aumentó de 100 a 180 del año 0 al año 1, un aumento del 80%. Del año 1 al año 2, el número de conejos aumentó de 180 a 324, un aumento del 80%. La tasa de crecimiento para esta población de conejos es del 80%. El interés, expresado como porcentaje, es una tasa de crecimiento. Para un patrón de crecimiento exponencial con un factor de crecimiento b, la tasa de crecimiento es $b - 1$.

scientific notation A short way to write very large or very small numbers. A number is in scientific notation if it is of the form $a \times 10^n$, where n is an integer and $1 \le a < 10$.

notación científica Una manera corta de escribir números muy grandes o muy pequeños. Un número está e notación científica si está en la forma $a \times 10^n$, donde n es un entero y $1 \le a < 10$.

standard form The most common way we express quantities. For example, 27 is the standard form of 3^3.

forma normal La manera más común de expresar una cantidad. Por ejemplo, 27 es la forma normal de 3^3.

Academic Vocabulary

The following terms are important to your understanding of the mathematics in this unit. Knowing and using these words will help you in thinking, reasoning, representing, communicating your ideas, and making connections across ideas. When these words make sense to you, the investigations and problems will make more sense as well.

D

decide To use the given information and any related facts to find a value or make a determination.
related terms: determine, find, conclude

Sample: Study the pattern in the table. Decide whether the relationship is linear or exponential.

x	−1	0	1	2	3
y	−9	−7	−5	−3	−1

Each y-value increases by 2 when each x-value increases by 1. The relationship is linear.

decidir Usar la información dada y cualesquiera datos relacionados para hallar un valor o tomar una determinación.
términos relacionados: determinar, hallar, concluir

Ejemplo: Estudia el patrón en la tabla. Decide si la relación es lineal o exponencial.

x	−1	0	1	2	3
y	−9	−7	−5	−3	−1

Cada valor de y aumenta en 2 cuando cada valor de x aumenta en 1. La relación es lineal.

describe To explain using details. You can describe a situation using words, numbers, graphs, tables, or any combination of these.
related terms: explain, tell, present, detail

Sample: Consider the following equations.

Equation 1: $y = 3x + 5$ Equation 2: $y = 5(3^x)$

Use a table to describe the change in y-values as the x-values increase in both equations.

x	0	1	2	3	4
$y = 3x + 5$	5	8	11	14	17
$y = 5(3^x)$	5	15	45	135	405

In y = 3x + 5, the value of y increases by 3 when x increases by 1. In y = 5(3^x), the value of y increases by a factor of 3 when x increases by 1.

describir Explicar usando detalles. Puedes describir una situación usando palabras, números, gráficas, tablas o cualquier combinación de éstos.
términos relacionados: explicar, decir, presentar, dar detalles

Ejemplo: Considera las siguientes ecuaciones.

Ecuación 1: $y = 3x + 5$ Ecuación 2: $y = 5(3^x)$

Usa una tabla para describir el cambio en los valores de y a medida que los valores de x se incrementan en ambas ecuaciones.

x	0	1	2	3	4
$y = 3x + 5$	5	8	11	14	17
$y = 5(3^x)$	5	15	45	135	405

In y = 3x + 5, el valor de y aumenta en 3 cuando x aumenta en 1. En y = 5(3^x), el valor de y aumenta por un factor de 3 cuando x aumenta en 1.

explain To give facts and details that make an idea easier to understand. Explaining something can involve a written summary supported by factual information, a diagram, chart, table, or any combination of these.

related terms: describe, justify, tell

Sample: **Etymologists are working with a population of mosquitoes that have a growth factor of 8. After 1 month there are 6,000 mosquitoes. In two months, there are 48,000 mosquitoes.**

Write an equation for the population after any number of months. Explain each part of your equation.

I first find the initial population of mosquitoes by dividing 6,000 by 8 to get 750. I can then model the population growth with the equation $y = 750(8^m)$, where 750 represents the initial population, 8 is the growth factor, m is the number of months, and y is the population of mosquitoes after m months.

explicar Dar hechos y detalles que hacen que una idea sea más fácil de comprender. Explicar puede implicar un resumen escrito apoyado por un diagrama, un gráfica, una tabla o cualquier combinación de éstos.

términos relacionados: describir, justificar, decir

Ejemplo: **Los entomólogos trabajan con una población de mosquitos que tiene un factor de crecimiento de 8. Después de 1 mes hay 6,000 mosquitos. En dos meses, hay 48,000 mosquitos.**

Escribe una ecuación para la población después de cualquier número de meses. Explica cada parte de tu ecuación.

Primero hallo la población inicial de mosquitos dividiendo 6,000 entre 8 para obtener 750. Luego puedo modelar el crecimiento de la población con la ecuación $y = 750(8^m)$, donde 750 representa la población inicial, 8 es el factor de crecimiento, m es el número de meses y y es la población de mosquitos luego de m meses.

P

predict To make an educated guess based on the analysis of real data.

related terms: estimate, expect

Sample: **Predict the ones digit for the expression 3^{11}.**

3^1	3
3^2	9
3^3	27
3^4	81
3^5	243
3^6	729
3^7	2187
3^8	6561

The pattern for the ones digit of the powers of 3 is 3, 9, 7, 1, as the exponent increases by 1. If I continue the pattern, 3^9 will end with a 3, 3^{10} will end with a 9, and 3^{11} will end with a 7.

predecir Hacer una conjetura informada basada en el análisis de datos reales.

términos relacionados: estimar, esperar

Ejemplo: **Predice el dígito de las unidades para la expresión 3^{11}.**

3^1	3
3^2	9
3^3	27
3^4	81
3^5	243
3^6	729
3^7	2187
3^8	6561

El patrón para el dígito de las unidades de las potencias de 3 es 3, 9, 7, 1, a medida que el exponente aumenta en 1. Si continúo el patrón, 3^9 terminará con un 3, 3^{10} terminará con un 9, y 3^{11} terminará con un 7.

Index

Area model, 5, 11, 29–30, 43, 48, 68

Algebra
- equation, 4, 5, 8, 10, 12, 13, 41, 61, 63, 65, 72, 76, 78
- exponent, 6, 12, 29, 61, 62, 64, 69, 72, 73
- exponential, 4–12, 14, 23, 32–34, 52, 59, 65, 66
- exponential relationship, 4, 9, 10, 19, 47, 59, 76, 78
- expression, 11, 64, 65, 68, 69
- function, 66
- graph, 4, 5, 12, 17, 19–21, 31, 39, 58, 66, 76–78
- growth rate, 35–46, 81
- line, 16, 30
- linear relationship, 4, 14, 15, 29, 58
- plot, 55
- point, 15, 27, 30, 39, 55
- slope, 16, 30
- variable, 16, 21, 26
- *y*-intercept, 16, 27–30, 32

Base
- definition, 6, 79
- two as a, 6–7, 59–60, 65

Calculator
- evaluating exponential expressions with, 6, 46
- graphing exponential equations, 63
- scientific notation and, 17, 70–71
- using, 6, 17, 46, 63, 64, 69–71

Check for reasonableness, 20, 64

Compare
- equations, 21, 25, 37, 51, 63, 78
- graphs, 9–10, 15, 21, 39, 50, 52, 53, 57, 63, 66, 73, 78
- tables, 53

Compound growth, 35–37
- ACE, 39–41, 43–46, 72
- definition, 37, 79
- equation for, 36–37, 39, 45, 72
- inflation rate, 40, 45, 72
- investing, 35–37, 39, 41, 45–46

Concrete model, *see* **Model**

Decay factor, 49–52
- ACE, 54–57
- decay rate and, 51
- definition, 49, 51, 79

Decay pattern, 48–52, 58, 74–75
- ACE, 53–57
- area and cuts, 48–49, 53, 77, 79
- breakdown of medicine, 50–51, 54
- cooling water, 51–52, 55
- linear, 53
- population, 67
- radioactive decay, 74–75

Decay rate, definition, 51, 79

Diagram, 5, 11–12, 29–30, 43, 48, 68

Equation
- ACE, 11–18, 24–31, 38–46, 53–57, 64–72
- comparing, 21, 25, 37, 51, 63, 78
- for compound growth, 36–37, 39, 45, 72
- for exponential decay, 49–52, 53–69, 72, 73, 75, 78
- for exponential growth, 6–10, 11–46, 59–64, 66, 73, 77–78
- graphing exponential, 7–9, 12–13, 15–16, 20–21, 23, 27–29, 31–32, 42, 49–55, 57–58, 63, 66, 73, 75, 77–78
- writing, 7, 9–10, 12–16, 18, 21, 23, 24–26, 28–31, 32, 34, 36–37, 38–39, 44–45, 49–50, 52, 53–57, 59, 61–62, 68–69, 71–72, 75, 76–77

Experiment
- cooling water, 51–52
- cutting ballots, 11
- half-life, 74–75

Exponent
- definition, 6, 80
- calculator key for, 6, 46
- negative, 69

Exponential decay, 48–52, 58, 74–75

ACE, 53–57
- definition, 49, 80
- equation for, 49–52, 53–69, 72, 73, 75, 78
- graph of, 50, 54
- halving, 48–49, 53
- rate, 50–52, 79

Exponential form, definition, 6, 80

Exponential growth, 5–47, 59–73, 76–78
- ACE, 11–18, 24–31, 38–46, 64–72
- definition, 8, 80
- doubling, 5–7, 12–13, 20–21, 77
- equation for, 6–10, 11–46, 59–64, 66, 73, 77–78
- fractional growth factors and, 33–37, 38–46, 47
- graph of, 8, 15, 23, 27–28, 30, 42, 66
- starting value and, 10, 47
- two as a base, 6–7, 59–60, 65
- whole number growth factors and, 5–32

Exponential relationship, definition, 8, 80

Glossary, 79–81

Graph, 7–10, 21, 23, 32, 42, 49–50, 52, 63, 73, 75–78
- ACE, 12–13, 15, 27–31, 57, 66
- comparing, 9–10, 15, 21, 39, 50, 52, 53, 57, 63, 66, 73, 78
- of exponential decay, 50, 54
- of exponential equations on a graphing calculator, 63
- of exponential growth, 8, 15, 23, 27–28, 30, 42, 66
- making, 7, 9, 12–13, 21, 31, 49, 52, 53, 55, 57, 63, 75, 76–77

Growth factor, 8–9, 20–23, 33–37, 47
- ACE, 11–18, 24–31, 38–46
- definition, 8, 81
- percent change and, 35–37, 40–41, 43–46, 47
- whole number, 5–32

Index

Acknowledgments

Team Credits

The people who made up the **Connected Mathematics 2** team—representing editorial, editorial services, design services, and production services—are listed below. Bold type denotes core team members.

Leora Adler, Judith Buice, Kerry Cashman, Patrick Culleton, Sheila DeFazio, Katie Hallahan, Richard Heater, **Barbara Hollingdale, Jayne Holman,** Karen Holtzman, **Etta Jacobs,** Christine Lee, Carolyn Lock, Catherine Maglio, **Dotti Marshall,** Rich McMahon, Eve Melnechuk, Kristin Mingrone, Terri Mitchell, **Marsha Novak,** Irene Rubin, Donna Russo, Robin Samper, Siri Schwartzman, **Nancy Smith,** Emily Soltanoff, **Mark Tricca,** Paula Vergith, Roberta Warshaw, Helen Young

Additional Credits

Diana Bonfilio, Mairead Reddin, Michael Torocsik, nSight, Inc.

Technical Illustration

WestWords, Inc.

Cover Design

tom white.images

Photos

2 t, Jacques Jangoux/Alamy; **2 b,** (ZF) Virgo/Corbis; **3 t,** Inga Spence/Visuals Unlimited; **3 b,** AP Photo/Chuck Burton; **13,** Dr. Stanley Flegler/Visuals Unlimited; **14,** Tim Pannell/Masterfile; **21,** Nicolas Granier/Peter Arnold, Inc.; **21 inset,** Jacques Jangoux/Alamy; **22,** Photodisc/Getty Images, Inc.; **23,** Sheldon, Allen Blake/Animals Animals-Earth Scenes; **25,** Wolfgang Kaehler/Corbis; **26,** David Young-Wolff/PhotoEdit; **33,** Steve Maslowski/Visuals Unlimited; **34,** Geoff Dann/Dorling Kindersley; **35,** Topham/The Image Works; **36 t,** (ZF) Virgo/Corbis; **36 b,** Steve Allen/AGE Fotostock; **38,** Michael Wickes/The Image Works; **40,** Creatas/AGE Fotostock; **41,** DK Limited/Corbis; **43,** David Young-Wolff/PhotoEdit; **44,** George Disario/Corbis; **48,** Tony Freeman/PhotoEdit; **52,** Richard Smith/Masterfile; **57,** Saxpix.com/AGE Fotostock; **61,** Richard Haynes; **65,** Richard Haynes; **69,** Tony Freeman/PhotoEdit; **71,** Design Pics Inc./Alamy

Data Sources

The water hyacinth data on page 2 is from "Killer Weed Strikes Lake Victoria" in The Christian Science Monitor, January 12, 1998, Volume 90, Number 32. Copyright © 1998 The Christian Science Monitor. All Rights Reserved.